CHAINED MAIL

Alan Nunn

MINERVA PRESS
LONDON
ATLANTA MONTREUX SYDNEY

CHAINED MAIL
Copyright © Alan Nunn 1998

All Rights Reserved

No part of this book may be reproduced in any form,
by photocopying or by any electronic or mechanical means,
including information storage or retrieval systems,
without permission in writing from both the copyright owner
and the publisher of this book.

ISBN 1 86106 884 0

First Published 1998 by
MINERVA PRESS
195 Knightsbridge
London SW7 1RE

Printed in Great Britain for Minerva Press

CHAINED MAIL

"To keep going the spirit that kept us going"

For my beloved wife, Eileen, who waited twenty months before receiving a postcard (already over a year old) saying I was a POW and who has never complained that in it I appeared to care more for my mother's cat than for her.

Acknowledgements

I wish to thank Mrs E. Hardie who has kindly given me permission to use her husband's drawing of the mountains round Takanun. As a POW he was medical officer in this and other camps on the Burma-Siam Railway, his experiences being published by the Imperial War Museum.

Also I thank my niece Grace Snape for typing this book so professionally.

This is a collection of letters that a POW in the Middle East would have liked to have sent to his brother

Preface

Fifty years have passed since these letters were written – letters written to my brother with no hope of being posted, and therefore, metaphorically chained in prison. Looking back to those wartime years I feel anyone reading them will find them more interesting if I add a word of explanation to my original introduction, which was written early in 1942.

Most of the letters were written within two or three weeks of the date they bear, and thus in genuine ignorance of what the future held. A few gaps were filled in later, but as they stand I believe they are literally, and literarily, unique.

One thing the letters do not make clear is the reason they were written: they were written to be published! The title was chosen at the beginning, and although, of necessity they were written in secret, I spent hours discussing book writing, authorship, style, etc. with my companions, which certainly made a change from chewing over our conditions, the possible date of release, the eternal subject of food, or the vicious criticism of our fellow POWs.

It was not an obsession but an absorbing new hobby, consciously taken up to help cope with the pressures around me. Something to give me an incentive in life that would mean survival, where many 'just gave up' and died.

I certainly wrote with the intention of seeing the letters published when I got home. Unfortunately, it took me a hundred days to achieve that, and I was well aware too many were ahead of me, and the market would be saturated. I then realised there was very little hope of success as the contents were not harrowing enough.

That is not surprising. Acting on the sensible principle of 'Never be first; never be last; and keep your head down', the nearest I came to personal violence (outside the Selarang episode) was when a Japanese guard found I had been using a six foot bamboo from our sleeping platform for a clothes line. He showed his official displeasure by tapping me on the head with it. Then, writing as I was under the noses of the Japanese there was much I was obliged to leave out, in case one of their periodic searches brought my work to light. I should have been in serious trouble, even if they had not bothered to read it. Had they read it and found it contained 'sensitive' material I could have been in dead trouble – literally! I did not fancy that!

After the war I thought of changing the title to *Book of Life*, which was very appropriate as I believe writing it helped in no small measure to keep me alive. I rejected this as it could have invited the charge of blasphemy from those who know it as the title of an important and very serious book mentioned in the last book of the Bible, and I did not want to give offence.

It was essential to keep a sense of humour if one was to survive, and I believe these letters show that. Fear and dread were pushed to the back of the mind as far as possible, so as not to dwell on them. If you read another notebook kept throughout my POW experiences you would find just the same humour coming through. I called this book *Cyclopaedia Nunnica*, being inspired by that most valuable book in a prison camp – *Pear's Cyclopaedia*, indispensable for those organising quizzes. That book shows how conscious we were of our years being wasted. It shows the craving for useful knowledge of any kind. From 'How to Play Bridge' to 'How to Preach Sermons'. From 'Notes on Topham's *Company Law*' to speaking German, Russian and Dutch.

The end of the war stimulated more notetaking, to make sure I remembered what happened. These and sundry other notes were collected into an exercise book entitled *Upon Release*. After all, we all learn from our experiences, and experiences need to be remembered accurately if we are to benefit from them; so those memories need to be as accurate as possible, especially if we are to share them with others.

Contents

Preface		ix
List of Illustrations		xvii
Introduction		xxi

Part One

One	The Capitulation	25
Two	One Week of Woe	35
Three	Tropical Habits	41
Four	Two Months	47
Five	The Rumpus	51
Six	Vitamised Vapours	54
Seven	The Discovery of Talent	59
Eight	Lines of Communication	67
Nine	The Red Cross	70
Ten	In Quest of Knowledge	73
Eleven	Selarang	79

Twelve	Change of Address	87
Thirteen	Casual Labour	93
Fourteen	Christmas 1942	100
Fifteen	Ring Out! Ye Bells!	103
Sixteen	Once I Built a Railroad	107
Seventeen	Fruit for Labour	121
Eighteen	Prince Bernhart's Birthday	136
Nineteen	Constant Companion	143
Twenty	The Activity of the Idle	153
Twenty-One	The Monsoon Breaks	161
Twenty-Two	Letters from Home	166
Twenty-Three	The Housing Problem	173
Twenty-Four	The Festive Season Once More	178
Twenty-Five	The Road to Japan	181
Twenty-Six	Alongside the Wharf	187
Twenty-Seven	A Break in Communications	191
Twenty-Eight	Everything is 'Sunda'	195
Afterthought (Commonly called 'Epilogue')		204

Part Two

	Upon Release	219
	Stories Told by Prisoners of War	253
Appendix	Cyclopaedia Nunnica: Summary	275
	'What a War'	278
	'A Mess Tin of Rice'	280

List of Illustrations

Original Introduction	19
'Send it by Rail'	50
'The Dhobi Place' signed Walter my nickname at the time	66
Certificate for first prize	74
The One That Got Away	93
Extract From Original Manuscript	106
The Railway I helped to Build	120
Membership Card of the Stedfast Club	159
Details of Membership	160
Section traced from Rangoon to Bangkok Railway	172
The Far Eastern Theatre showing my journey to Japan	186
Address and Admonition Given on Transportation of Prisoners of War	189
Mountains around Takanun	215

The Badge of the Mining Company at Ube	219
My Name in Japanese	220
Notice on Air Raid Shelter	221
Letter from the Swiss Consulate, Tokyo	226
Instructions received with the Swiss Consul's letter	227
Straws for working down the mine	230
Plan of the POW camp at Ube	236
Southern Japan	252

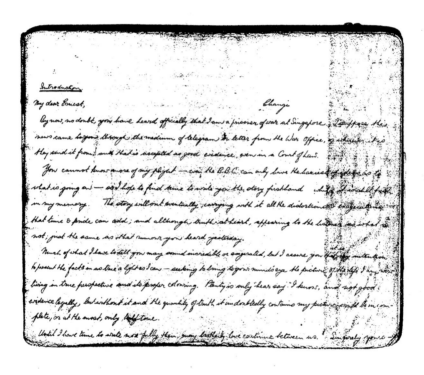

The Introduction from the Original Manuscript

Introduction

Roberts Barracks, Changi

My dear Ernest,

By now, no doubt, you will have heard officially that I am a prisoner of war at Singapore. I suppose the news came through the medium of telegram or letter from the War Office, or wherever it is they send it from; and that is accepted as good evidence even in a court of law.

You cannot know more of my plight... even the BBC can only have the haziest of ideas as to what is going on... so I hope to find time to write you the story first hand, while it is still fresh in my memory. The story will out eventually, carrying with it all the distortion and exaggerations that time and pride can add, and although true at heart, appearing to the listener as that which is not, just like that rumour you heard yesterday.

Much of what I have to tell you may sound incredible or exaggerated, but I assure you that it is my intention to present the facts in as true a light as I can, seeking to bring to your mind's eye the picture of the life I am now living in true perspective and in its proper colouring. Plenty is only 'hearsay', I know, and not good evidence legally; but without the quantity of truth it undoubtedly contains my picture would be incomplete, or at the most only in half-tone.

Until I have time to write more fully then, may brotherly love continue between us.
Sincerely yours,
Alan

Part One

Chapter One

The Capitulation

Changi, 27 February 1942

My dear Ernest,

February 15 was the day we packed up – I don't expect you knew that till some days later. It was a Sunday, and a most unholy day it seemed when it dawned. Even now I can see the little caretaker's room adjoining the large joinery workshop, with the early light of morn filtering through the shutters and the underside of the table beneath which I spent the night, getting what sleep I could. I was not alone in that room; there must have been five or six others there, nerves all to pieces, like myself cowering from the shells that fell around us.

You cannot know what it is like to be under shellfire, Ernest, having been fortunate enough to stay in England throughout the war. You've had the bombing, I know, and that is plenty bad enough; but even that is not as bad as the shelling. One can hear the planes above, perhaps even see them; can tell within a short time when the bombs will come. For a few awful seconds you are in a veritable Hell, then the explosions indicate that it is all over. But with shelling there are no planes to pass over. Perhaps the first thing you hear is the shell whistling slowly through the air towards you, sounding for all the world like a generator that has just been switched off, and which is losing speed. It sounds as though it has insufficient momentum to keep it aloft, and you know it will not land very far away. If you are already down on the ground you try to shrink to nothing and brace yourself for the explosion.

While busy strengthening the air raid shelter in which I had particular interest, I was walking across an asphalt yard when a shell took me very much by surprise. It sizzled down viciously and hit the ground less than ten yards beyond me. I was only half way down to the ground when it burst and I felt a small piece of something hit me in the arm. I got up and scuttled for safety like a rabbit, measuring my length at least once more as I heard another shell landing. That shell which nearly landed on top of me laid out three Indian soldiers who were just as far away as I was, but just beyond the point at which the shell landed. Fortunately for me, all the blast went forward. That was the narrowest escape I had. My arm was not really hurt, I'm glad to say: there was only a small puncture in the skin.

One of our number was buried alive while sheltering in a slit trench we had dug in the cemetery adjoining the ground on which the timber workshop stood. Fortunately he was not badly hurt, but after this incident we were not keen on remaining in our slit trenches. That was why this particular Sunday found about twenty of us building a pukka shelter in the workshop. When there was a lull in the firing, eight of us would hurry out to a pile of timber, seize a long beam, and frantically drag it back to the safety of the building. Once under cover, the beam was quickly sawn in half and placed in position.

I was glad to be doing something I can tell you. Up till then I had lived the life of a frightened rabbit, hiding in my burrow and only coming up for food. Such a life, under such conditions plays havoc with the nerves, Ernest. Those who know would tell you that when you have a job to do, you forget the danger you are in and get on with it. If you sit tight doing nothing, all you have to do is to think of the shells and long for the whole affair to finish.

We were still working in the afternoon when one of our officers appeared on the scene, obviously with some announcement to make. When silence was at last established inside the building (we could not arrange for the noise outside to stop) he came out with these startling words: 'The battle of Singapore finishes at four o'clock this afternoon.'

We did not understand at first that we had surrendered. I distinctly remember wondering what on earth had made the Japs decide to finish the battle – they certainly seemed to have plenty of ammunition left.

That last hour and a half was worse than all the days that had gone by. Hope, which had buoyed us up for so long and helped us to stick it, was gone. It was useless to think that very soon we would receive those long promised planes and begin to turn the tables on our foes, for we were beaten. Tempers, already badly frayed, flared out, and everybody sought an outlet for the pent-up passion they suddenly found within. Arms and equipment proved an excellent outlet and suffered severely. The destroyers derived satisfaction from the knowledge that they were striking a last blow for England. There was plenty of whisky about and those in favour of a 'scorched earth' policy disposed of the stuff successfully – at the risk of their sobriety.

One lad had been rather vindictive, I remember, and while calling the Japs rather nasty names that I wouldn't like to repeat, he advocated that the gramophone should be smashed to prevent it falling into their hands. What the Japs would want it for I couldn't quite understand.

The Japs seemed keen on making a grand finale, for they started giving us everything they had got. The shells still sounded uncomfortably close when my troop commander appeared on a motor bike. He wanted me to follow him somewhere and ordered me to prepare to move. I felt most insubordinate at that moment.

He must have been in a hurry to get back, for, as soon as he saw I was in motion and clear of the other vehicles, he set off at a good speed without bothering to look behind.

What a sight I saw as I tore along! I was amazed, for I had not left the cemetery for days. Everywhere was chaos and desolate confusion. The road was littered with scraps of masonry while volumes of smoke rolled up from fires on either side. Here, the trolley-bus wires were down, making the carnage look still worse, and as my lorry bumped over them I wondered if they would catch up round my wheels. There was a blazing lorry in the middle of a field with the angry red flames surmounted by volumes of black smoke. A burning ammunition dump added greyness to the scene and the explosions caused me to jump. I wondered if it was the enemy at first, as I drove along, hanging on to the wheel and gritting my teeth as though my very life depended on it.

I passed another blazing lorry, this time outside a factory. I noticed how fiercely the tyres were burning. Smoke and noise were everywhere and it was impossible to visualise the scene as it had been a week ago.

The motorcyclist stopped, and dismounting he turned towards me. To my horror I saw he was not my officer, and I realised I had followed the wrong man! I hastily turned round, in my agitation taking more locks on the wheel than necessary, and hurried back the way I had come.

A shell burst in a field on my off side and not far in front. I saw the vivid red flash through the murk, and that was enough! I pulled up, dived out, and ducking round under the tailboard, descended in a heap in the deep open monsoon drain on the near side, leaving my engine running.

The shells were coming far too close, and I crawled along until I reached the cover of the tunnel where the drain went under the road. My watch showed me the time was 3.15 p.m. Three quarters of an hour to go before the ceasefire. I felt that the time for heroics was over, and I determined to stay where I was until things quietened down. I was as safe as possible where I was, for the drain curved behind me and another fellow was between me and the opening. The road above me was strong enough to protect me from a direct hit. What was more, the drain was dry.

The minutes dragged slowly by: still half an hour to go! 'Aircraft overhead!' cried someone, then Swish-h-h-h! as the bombs come down. I breathed freely again as I heard them explode a good way off, little realising that four of my comrades had been killed by those selfsame bombs.

Four o'clock passed without any reduction in the noise. Gradually the firing died down and we ventured out. I returned to the cemetery and reported to the major.

The day dragged on. Near us a field gun still fired, the badly rammed shells spinning over our heads with a vicious whizz! Later, we were told the layer had to be shot because he refused to leave his post. He was loading, laying and firing the gun by himself, and we were afraid that he was inciting the Japs to reply.

Up above twenty-seven aircraft droned – they always came over like that. They were flying at a great height. To our horror we heard a 'Beaufor' open up and a couple of white puffs of smoke appeared among them as if by magic. Then came that sound which we knew so well – rather like gravel being tipped from a cart to my way of thinking – the swish-h-h-h of falling bombs. Twenty-seven plane loads were released all together, falling indiscriminately on the town below. Down on my stomach I went again, while close by I could hear a comrade beseeching God and Mary to stop it all.

As the sun sank down to his rest a silence descended that was both blissful and holy. It seemed so unnatural, and such a relief after all the terror and noise of the past week.

An order had come through from somewhere saying that we must wear something white on our hats – what humiliation it was having to show the white feather!

When it was dark, excitement started to run high. Already rumour had been busily at work, and the move we were about to make was alternately authorised by the Japs and issued secretly by some high British officer. We were going to the docks, we knew, but the story was that the whole capitulation was a mistake, and we were to be either evacuated or re-equipped under cover of night. We understood there was a colossal conference going on in the Union Jack Club, which was the new HQ.

We moved without lights and while it was very dark. We moved fast too. That journey stands out in my memory as the craziest I know. I had to drive recklessly over bomb and shell craters and scattered masonry, or through trolley-bus wires, festooned from their standards, at a speed I never hope to achieve again under such conditions. The blackness, assisted by the smoke of several fires, was accentuated by the leaping flames that devoured a building on our road. A length of cable caught round my truck and I had to stop to clear it out of the way. Desperately I tugged at the wire while the truck I was following receded into the distance.

At last the front was cleared, but one end of the wire was fast round my back axle. We went on, overtaking the three trucks that had passed us, to regain our place in the column – such reckless driving!

I think even you would have crossed your fingers and held your breath if you had been beside me.

We arrived in one piece, however, closely followed by fifty feet of cable which had dragged noisily behind, occasionally jolting us when a following vehicle ran over it.

Arrival at the seafront meant question time. Thousands of cars and lorries had parked there, and all the occupants wanted to know what had happened. I will not weary you with every report I heard, for as fast as I tried to confirm one rumour at another source, I had another story offered, with the earnest assurance that it was authentic and to be accepted in good faith. Subsequent events proved those reports which told that we should *not* be evacuated, *nor* re-equipped, and that we should meekly submit ourselves to the Japs, proved to be true.

We were herded into an open space (or square as one would term it, being in the middle of a city) and told to bed down as best we could for the night. My major told me to leave my truck where it was, because two or three lorries were treading on its tail, and I could not move it. We were only going a couple of hundred yards, so it seemed certain that it would be safe until the morning.

During the night, a fire broke out rather too close to be pleasant, and we decamped to another part of the town. In the morning I went back for my lorry; but bless you,

Ernest, it had disappeared into thin air! It had gone: wire and all, along with all my kit and a useful pile of grub.

A comrade of mine, Jonnie by name, and I looked hopefully in all directions for something on four wheels which might conceivably be our wagon. We saw a deserted looking motor cycle at the side of the road and enlisted its aid in our search; but it was fruitless, and we returned, disappointed, to our rendezvous, I consoling myself with the thought that I had, at any rate, had the sense to transfer my small pack (in which were all my valuables) to the wagon in which I had last travelled after deserting my own. Alas! false hope! When I came to get my washing gear I found to my horror that the haversack was somebody else's that I had picked up in mistake.

I'll leave you to imagine my feelings when I discovered my loss. All my kit, all those little things I had learnt to value, the little Bible that Maurice had rebound, all those souvenirs I had picked up, including some postage stamps: all gone with the wind, so to speak!

Don't let me dwell on my misfortunes, however, or make me tell that bitter story to the end! We waited about for half the day (which provided us with an excellent opportunity to go looting in the houses of civilians who had had to leave everything behind) and then returned to our base in the cemetery, postal address Hallifax Rd (good old Yorkshire). I was glad about this as I had dumped some of my kit there before we left. I had not done any looting, and apart from what I stood up in, my sole possessions were an 'Aussie' hat and a small bag containing a towel, a bar of soap and a tin of talcum powder.

The only other thing of note that day was an order to put our watches forward about two hours to conform to Japanese time.

That night I slept in the cemetery, my sleep being disturbed not by ghosts, as you might suppose, but by a woman screaming in a most hair-raising way. What was happening I don't know, but it sounded as if some man (whose voice I could hear as well) was forcing her to do something, or go somewhere that she did not want to. The language was not English but it was obvious the poor woman was getting the worse of it. There was nothing I could do about it – it might have been a Japanese soldier having a night out, and if I had interfered it might have been very bad for me.

We were up early next day as we were to march the fifteen miles to Changi. In spite of this it was four o'clock in the afternoon before word came through for us to move.

We set off, carrying our kit with us. Mine had swollen to a small haversack on my back and the aforesaid little bag (a 'civvy' gas mask carrier in reality) both crammed as full as could be. Although space was so limited you will be surprised to hear that I was carrying three books I had selected from a pile dumped in the cemetery. I told others to take some, as I felt sure they would come in useful if we are to be prisoners for any length of time.

There is not much to tell of that march. It raised large blisters on my feet, the tenderness of which is still with me. I can still see several scenes that we passed, however, which are so vivid that I must tell you about them.

There was the Indian with a large hole in his head lying near a tree on our left. We passed two cows in a field, blown up like balloons with their legs pointing to the sky and creating the most frightful stench. The village of Paya Lebar had Jap flags stuck on every door, some nothing more than a small scrap of paper on which a red ball had been scribbled in red pencil. In the road was a burnt out car. I peered into it and saw the charred remains of two bodies, the heads and shoulders of which were missing.

On we marched, weary and hot, past an ambulance that had broken down days before and which was a landmark to me who had travelled that road frequently in my truck.

It would be a crime not to mention the kindness of the villagers at Teck Hock. They came out with pails of water to fill our mugs and bottles as we passed. We did not realise the full value of this until we arrived at Changi. Then we found just how serious the shortage of water was.

We arrived. Yes Ernest, we arrived, but well after midnight had passed. Need I say we were whacked? It was hard work to go for the scanty meal provided. Any place on the floor was good enough for sleeping, and I assure you, there was not much talking that night.

Love to all

Alan

Chapter Two

One Week of Woe

Changi, 9 March 1942

My dear Ernest,

Looking back, as I do now from the first day in our new camp, those first days after our arrival at Changi seem scarcely more realistic than a nightmare. Not that I doubt their existence for a single moment, for I still have the remains of those great big blisters I picked up on the march. The bad condition of my feet kept me off them for a fortnight, and getting about was far too painful, so you can imagine how displeased I was to be marshalled into the top storey of one of the tall barrack buildings that are quite common in that part of the world, whose postal address is Roberts Barracks, Changi.

To make matters worse, the roof had been interfered with by a bomb and sagged drunkenly in the middle on the near side, cutting off a quarter of our floor space. Shutters, doors, and blinds had ceased to exist, so when it rained and the wind blew hard, it was difficult to find a dry spot. There was one great compensation... we were pretty free from the flies and 'skeeters' that plagued the folk downstairs.

'In what lies the nightmare?' I think I hear you ask. Certainly not in my feet or the buildings. They were far too tangible for that. It lay mostly in the men, my comrades, who lived around me and who were still showing the effects of those last few days of war. Men who are now back to normal and the same in mind and temper as I had known them in Ireland. During that first woeful week they were scarcely recognisable with their frayed tempers and ragged nerves. I suppose I appeared the same to them, so I must not criticise. Then there was the scarcity of food. We had brought several truckloads with us, and this was rationed to us until the Japs could organise our food supply.

We did not quite starve, although there is not one below the rank of quartermaster or cook who had nearly enough. Half a dozen biscuits and a little corned beef hash was all we had to fill us on more than one day.

The first week produced an amazing crop of rumours; foremost among which were those which told we were soon to have an issue of rice – each man was to be allowed one and an impossible fraction of an ounce.

The rice arrived, and I am glad to say it was in greater quantities than at first expected. But how little it seemed, and how anxiously we lined up for more! There were more than a few who drew their grub and walked straight to the back of the queue, standing there to eat their meagre helping. If they were lucky they got a miserably small second helping.

There were plenty of flavouring materials, however, and some experiments in this direction were attended with great success. Cheese, curry, and salt were good, while the chocolate rice made from Emergency Rations was looked upon as second only to 'bully' rice.

Food was our only thought, for we never felt full, and as if that was not bad enough, we tortured ourselves by conjuring up visions of those lovely dishes we had at home, in days when there was plenty, and rice pudding could be eschewed. Oh our poor stomachs, how they gnawed!

All this time I had been condemned by the MO to keeping off my feet as much as possible. Indeed, I was glad to do so, for the blisters on my feet were not easily forgotten; besides, there was plenty of work to be done, putting our quarters shipshape. I was pleased to miss the work, but, oh my poor feet when I had to hobble down all those stairs to get my grub from the cookhouse! Then there was the return journey up all those stairs with my precious food. Anyone here will tell you what a job that was, even when your feet are not bad. We had no energy Ernest! I had to pull myself up by the handrail like an invalid downstairs the first time for a fortnight.

There was very little water, and even less to drink. A muddy stream gave us the wherewithal to wash, while more than one bottle of water could only be obtained by the greatest guile.

Everything was topsy-turvy. Everybody was on top of one another, and nobody was happy. The only gleam of sunshine in a very dull sky was that everybody had a good supply of cigarettes.

A few days showed some sort of order taking shape, although the medical officer said dysentery had broken out and was cause for anxiety.

More work was provided by the digging and fly-proofing of latrines. None of your Scout camp affairs, Ernest, but ten feet deep at the minimum and several yards long. As soon as was possible these were covered over with lidded seats 'claimed' to be fly proof. How such affairs can boast such a claim beats me, for the continual opening and shutting of the lids defeats the principle to a great extent. Still, even I could see they were much better than nothing.

I'll say no more about the conditions under which we lived during that first week as prisoners of war except to point out, that at my reckoning, there were fifteen thousand of us collected into the comparatively small area covered by Robert's Barracks, the normal peacetime complement of which would be not more than three thousand. Believe me, when I tell you that peace and quiet were impossible.

Do you think fifteen thousand a high estimate? I go on the 'official' figures given by our major. The number of prisoners taken on the island amounted to sixty-two thousand, of which thirty thousand were British and Australian. The Aussies were in another barracks and the Indian troops were somewhere else.

You'll be wondering how I survived these days, especially as I was condemned to idleness by my bad feet. That I did so, and that almost cheerfully, is due to the fact that I was able to keep myself occupied all the time. I discovered I had a small scale map of England from a diary in my pocket, and my first amusement was to draw a map of Yorkshire. The reason for this was that I have always been very muddleheaded over the position of Huddersfield in relation to Manchester and Sheffield; and I felt duty bound to Eileen to make some attempt to unravel the mystery.

When I had finished it I noticed a neighbour energetically engaged on some woodcarving with very sorry looking results. The bug bit, and I found myself settling down to a name plate for the old house. Ambition to make something good produced an elaborate design, which I find is rather complicated now I have come to carving it with only a jack knife to help. It's not finished yet and I am still working on it.

To add seasoning to our amusements we had a most entertaining crop of rumours. Within this first week we heard that *Hengest* and *Horsa* (or whatever the boats bottled up in Brest are called – I know one is 'Gn' something and the other is 'Sch' ditto, but have no idea how to spell them) had escaped and sailed up the Channel, bringing down forty-two of our 'planes' *en passant*. We heard also that for some unknown reason Mr Churchill had resigned – I suppose that was because the Russians are doing so well that they have given the Germans a month to lay down their arms. According to some 'reliable' sources, Adolf is suing for a separate peace with Russia while he has been unsuccessfully flinging two invading forces at England's shores.

You will observe that we have plenty of variety; we just pay our money and take our choice.

Of course, we all deny that we believe them, and then go away kidding ourselves that the good news is true and the bad mere fabrication.

So much for the first week of life as a prisoner of war – POW for short, as can be seen from any of the notices put up around the camp.

Since then, things have settled down considerably. The officers have had to take their pips and crowns off their shoulders, and only wear one pip on the breast pocket. They wear the other pip within, and feel very sore about it, although our major (who is 6 ft 5 inches tall) summoned up enough humour to suppose the reason for this order was the Japs are so short that they cannot see pips put on epaulettes.

Yesterday we had to leave our top floor flat (no modern conveniences) and emigrate to the open about a quarter of a mile away. Carrying my kit in two journeys upset my feet again, just when they were on the verge of getting better. That is going to put me out of action again for a bit longer.

I've not had time to look round our new home properly, so I cannot describe it to you yet. One thing is certain, however, and that is now we are camping out, we have unlimited supplies of fresh air. That is one very good thing seeing we are so overcrowded. Another good thing is that the Japs seem content to let us (at least, me) stew in our own juice. This is good, as we have to salute all Japanese soldiers on sight; and that, I assure you, is a very bad thing, and to be avoided as much as conveniently possible. Who on earth wants to salute them!

Love to all

Alan

Chapter Three
Tropical Habits

Changi, 25 March 1942

My dear Ernest,

   More than a month has gone past since the ceasefire sounded, and we are beginning to settle down to our life as prisoners of war. Mind you, it's only for a month or so, as every other fellow here will tell you. When we get home we shall have a story that should take the stage in drawing-room or public bar for many an evening.

   We are now under canvas, and life is more precarious than on the top floor of a barrack block. At the moment, the clerk of the weather has an unfortunate habit of emptying several clouds full of moisture each day on to our particular part of Mother Earth, without being too careful over whether the tap is turned on too hard. We like the rain because it means we can have a shower bath, but we don't like it in such quantities that it fills our gutters and floods out our tents.

   This tropical habit is striking. The gay sunshine quickly disappears, and the clouds blow up. An hour later and in brilliant sunshine you may be left to re-arrange the happy home (the contents of which you may have hastily endeavoured to place above the high-tide mark) and sweep the flood from your door.

Not a day passes but we see lightning and hear thunder, even though the storm does not come near us, and our sky may be clear. Sometimes the storm does pass over us, and then we can hear the lightning flicker as it traces its forky patterns. Then the thunder is very loud, and amazing to tell, you can hear it tumbling across from one side of the sky to the other above your head.

But to come back to earth – like a little drop of rain. Our chief complaint at the moment is that we are always hungry. I eat every particle of rice I can get but even that does not suffice. This rice is awkward stuff, Ernest, to say the least of it. I go and get a plate full, and perhaps wangle a little extra from somebody else, and pack it away down the long red lane. I still want to eat, although I feel as tight as a drum. An hour later my stomach feels empty, and I start thinking of what I could do to a really square meal.

Rice has a nasty habit of turning to water once it's inside you. This is very good when it allows you to miss the 'delightful aroma' of the latrines for at least a week, but very inconvenient when it calls you from your bed three or four times during the night.

These nocturnal excursions have enabled me to study the stars. The Milky Way straggles across the sky with a brightness I never expected. Orion, the Pleiades, the Plough, and Cassiopia stand out magnificently in the cloudless sky. So do plenty of other stars but I don't know their names. I wish I had a map of the Heavens so that I could identify them.

The Pole Star is too low in the sky to be seen, but, judging from Orion and the Plough, my tent is facing North. When I wake up in the night I try to tell the time by the stars by noticing how far round they have turned.

What surprises me is the size of the Plough and Cassiopia. They sprawl across the northern sky, taking up two or three times the space they occupy when viewed from dear old England. Conversely, when I look at Orion, I find it more compact and only about half the size I am used to.

To the south I have found a cross of some description, but to my mind it seems too dim to be the Southern Cross. I cannot think what else it can be, but it's very disappointing.

The way I am writing this must suggest to you that my head is in the clouds, but I assure you that is not so. My stomach insists that I am still living in a hard hard world in which one requires to eat.

Yes Ernest, eat! even if it is only rice. It's surprising how many different kinds of rice there are. We have had several different kinds already. Some go gluey when cooked, other sorts go dry and crumble grain from grain. We have had ordinary rice, black rice (the best), stinking rice and limed rice. I can eat them all except the limed rice, it's the worst stuff I've ever encountered.

The first time we were given limed rice to eat, somebody thought the yellowish colour was due to mixing a few eggs with it. It might have accounted for the doubtful smell, and if the eggs were bad, for the more than doubtful taste. Eggs are eggs, and hard to come by at present, and I for one accepted this explanation and queued up for more which I heroically ate. Perhaps you can imagine my horror on looking at the fish knife I was using instead of a spoon, and finding it tarnished almost black! I had visions of a tarnished stomach lining and hoped for the best.

The flavour became stronger, and consequently, more objectionable. I thought of the tarnish, and decided that I could not eat it. Hunger was the better part of valour this time. What is limed rice? I don't know, but I have an idea that the lime is added to preserve it from rats and things while it is laying in store. The great problem is how to get rid of the lime.

Before I close, there is one subject which I must mention. If it did not follow the laws of supply and demand so closely, I would put it down as another tropical habit, this time on the part of the local inhabitants: to bleed the white man whiter. Trading with the natives is strongly discouraged and even strictly forbidden by the Japs. Even so, those with money to spend and tummies to fill have managed to get through the barbed wire surrounding our camp and buy things from the natives. You will hardly believe the racket it has become. Literally hundreds of men are staking their lives (for that is the penalty for being outside the wire and talking to the natives) against a few tins of food and a packet of fags.

I have not gone myself – whether through lack of nerve, or because of the high prices that are being asked, I do not know – but I hear quite a lot about it from those who have. Some of them bring the goods back into the camp and sell them to their comrades and make a profit on the deal by charging a higher price still.

The prices have risen quicker than a sky rocket. A tin of fish will now cost you from two to three dollars. Milk and Bully have both touched the five and even the six dollar mark. Cigarettes have risen to a dollar for ten unless you are lucky. Sugar, flour and butter cost dollars for absurdly small quantities. In fact, unless you have ten dollars in your pocket it is hardly worth going. When I tell you that the Malayan dollar is (or was) worth 2s 4d you can see how much some fellows are paying for a feed.

The lads at Changi here will not forget the black market in a hurry, I assure you.

There is another habit some folk out here have, and which it has only just occurred to me may be of interest. It is that of blowing bugles and trumpets very early in the morning. Of course, this is not a tropical habit as you can find it in any army camp but as I lie in bed near the open tent door I hear the different calls sounding from different parts of the camp. There is the usual army Reveille that starts 'Get out of bed, get out of bed'. Then there is the more unusual 'Charlie, Charlie, get out of bed', with an intriguing twiddly bit, on the 'bed', that some regiments use instead. Of course I could easily recognise the Royal Artillery trumpeter sounding our particular call, while further away in the distance the bagpipes skirled the Jocks out of bed. So you see, we have not completely lost our identity yet, even though the Japs make many rules and regulations. Although reveille is a very unpopular call, I must say there is an entrancing beauty in these calls as they come softly through the morning air laden with the promise of another glorious day. But then I am fortunate – I am not near enough to have one of the calls blared in my ear just when I want another five minutes.

It's time I closed down but before I do I must tell you one or two rumours floating around. I was almost prepared to believe that Germany had packed in three days ago. Everybody was talking about it, and there was a stir throughout the camp.

The lights of London were reported on for the first time on March 12th. Then we heard that Queen Mary had died. Later we had this amended to the *Queen Mary* being torpedoed but not sunk.

Various prophecies have sprung into being, some attributed to Spiritualists in the camp, as to the date on which we will find ourselves free. You can even hear the names of the boats on which we will travel home!

That Singapore will be declared an open town in the near future receives strong support in some quarters, but who can tell how much credit to give to these stories? I don't know where all the news comes from, or who it is, even that makes it up.

Love to all

Alan

Chapter Four

Two Months

Roberts Hospital, Changi, 20 April 1942

My dear Ernest,

Two months have passed and we are still POWs. Two months of our lives have been lost in the shape of enforced idleness and purposeless existence. But for me it is not as purposeless now as it was at first, for I have been absorbed into the machinery of that merciful institution known as a hospital.

On the first of April I received marching orders and was told, along with about two hundred other men to report to Roberts Hospital. Once there, we were settled into huts and marshalled into various parties for work connected with the hospital. I'm not going to start telling you a long account of the wonderful and glorious work that is going on at Roberts, or the inconceivable difficulties under which this is being carried on. After only three weeks here I am convinced that little will be left untold when we are free. I feel that, at the moment, you must be more interested in one little cog in some obscure corner of the works than to want my ramblings on the subject of the works themselves.

I was put on 'dhobi-ing' with a fair sized gang of fellows. Twice a day we loaded a trolley with inconceivably dirty linen of all descriptions and pushed it down the railway line to the sea. There we washed it in true Indian style, bashing the clothes on rocks and in the water until we knew they were well soaked. Often the things came back dirtier than they went, but as no one seemed to worry, neither did we. Nor could we do much about it when the rain prevented us putting them out to dry, and the bundles of damp linen were perforce left to rot. So much for the job I was doing. I had more interest in what was to fill my stomach before I attempted such work.

The improvement in our food had been greater than any had dared to hope for. Our three meals of rice a day outside the hospital had increased to four, and dinner was more like a meal than anyone had seen for a few weeks. I could hardly believe my eyes when I saw the size of the meat 'duffs' we sometimes got. I would have considered myself fortunate with a quarter of a portion. That we were feeding better was evident to me, as I found it necessary to make more regular trips to the latrine than the once a week that had previously sufficed.

I feel that I am better off than I was before. I get as good meals as anywhere and a home where I have a chance of settling down. Most of the lads in my unit have gone working down at Singapore, so I don't know when I shall see them again, or how unsettled a life they are now living.

Lately we have been having an issue of cigarettes, which has come as a boon to most fellows. Everybody I know has just about finished their store of several hundred which they grabbed on capitulation, and although the fags hardly last till next day, they are keenly looked for.

For myself, I have been able to turn my cigarettes to good account. Ten of them obtained for me half a tin of Vegemite the other day, but I am very grieved to have to say that I had it pinched after two days, and before I had time to eat it all.

Five cigarettes obtained me a useful notebook in which I keep various notes that interest me. Every issue day I receive many offers of 'duffs' or pasties, for as low as two cigarettes. It's wonderful how men will rather forgo their food than a smoke.

Fags find a place in the money market too. I can sell ten for one dollar with a clear conscience. Once I sold four cigarettes for fifty cents. The highest price I ever saw was two dollars for ten! It makes you think, when they should not be more than about ten cents a packet.

Well Ernest, the rumours continue to indicate good news from Russia and Libya. Those about this part of the world have not been too bad either. Two big naval battles have concluded in our favour with disastrous effect to the Jap Navy, so I suppose I shall be free soon. Most of us are pretty optimistic. I hope to be home by Christmas to tell you all my experiences.

Love to all

Alan

Send it by Rail

Chapter Five

The Rumpus

Roberts Hospital, Changi, 12 May 1942

My dear Ernest,

Things cannot run smooth for very long, can they? Here we are settling down to work in one place instead of being marched to Singapore to be at the beck and call of the Japs, doing whatever jobs they can find for us to do, and then comes the 'Rumpus'.

It started over two weeks ago with a complaint about the food.

In the RA hut we had several fellows whose tongues were beyond their control. On their own admission even, some of them had been sent to the Hospital Area because their own units preferred their room to their company. To put it bluntly, we had a rather tough crowd in our midst in the RA hut. And tough guys can turn very awkward and make a lot of mischief, believe me. As I said before, it all started over the food.

Our messing representative annoyed the powers that be by his violent and inconsiderate attacks, which, while voicing the mind of the whole hut, grossly misrepresented the actual feeling.

Then came complaints over the work and other matters, with counter-complaints over our conduct. Feeling ran extremely high, I can tell you.

Our lads asked for a change of job, as had been promised, and then grumbled because the change was from dhobi-ing to digging, which was much harder.

I don't want you to think that we all grumbled. Oh no! The RA is not completely composed of hooligans. Unfortunately a dozen black sheep can make the whole fifty muddy if they try hard enough.

The matter came to a head after a 'conflab' between our sergeant in charge and the officer in charge of fatigue parties that took place about a week ago. To our astonishment we were told that on Sunday (10 May) we were all going back to our units – lock, stock and barrel, but minus the sergeant and four men from his own regiment.

Such an arrangement as this was obviously unfair as some of the best workers in the camp, and who had never bleated a complaint, fell under the axe of this order.

Two of these worked on the dhobi party with me and we had become great friends. 'Todd' was my chief chess opponent and Jack was a rattling good fellow. The three of us decided that we did not want to quit, and that it was worth a fight to see if we could stay, so we ran to the officer in charge of the dhobi party and told him our troubles. He went to the colonel for backing and then gave those of us on his party orders not to move. The other party, however, would have nothing to do with verbal orders and went one better by sticking up a notice – you know the sort of thing – 'The undermentioned men will' etc., etc., upon which our names featured.

We rose to the occasion and countered with written instructions to remain, signed by a colonel RAMC. The notice to quit was only signed by a captain RA.

At this stage the fight passed out of our hands and I understand the officers got together and had it out amongst themselves. The captain RA was soundly ticked off by another colonel RAMC, but he succeeded in convincing that gentleman that even if it was a dirty trick, he was acting within his rights, and we should be allowed to quit, as per order.

Meanwhile, I had been looking to my second line of defences. I went to see the major in charge of my unit and asked for permission to remain and take the place of one of the relieving party, for every unit had to find replacements for the men being returned.

It was well that I did so, for the battle had gone against us and the marching orders we had received were allowed to stand.

I asked for an interview with the captain RA and produced written evidence of the permission. Captain RA looked at the sergeant RA with an inquiring glance – as much as to say 'Is this one of the quiet ones? Is he all right?' The sergeant RA nodded assent.

That's how it comes about that I am still in the hospital now that the others have gone, and the rumpus has ended. Poor Todd and Jack had to go and I hear they are booked for the march to Singapore in a day or so.

In the meantime I have a crop of new faces to inspect and a set of new personalities to review.

Love to all

Alan

Chapter Six
Vitamised Vapours

Roberts Hospital, 27 May 1942

My dear Ernest,

I suppose you have never worried your head over what a 'vitamin' is, have you? Not even when doing Organic Chemistry. Until recently, I never got beyond using the word when I wanted to appear scientific and impress people that one thing or another was good for them to eat. Lately I have been giving this subject a deal of thought. In fact, everybody in my little world has been giving the matter thought – it's the fashion.

It all started when they brought in to the hospital two or three men suffering from beri-beri and established a beri-beri ward. Within a day the whole camp was asking, 'What is beri-beri?'

The answers, although varied, all blamed it on to rice – eating too much rice, eating undercooked rice, eating rice husks, eating little bacteria that have found their way into the rice, were only a few.

Gradually the picture cleared and we saw that if rice is to be blamed, it is because it lacks something, and not because of any malignant qualities it possesses. In short, beri-beri is due to nothing more or less than a shortage of vitamin B. Apparently the rice we knew in England contains none.

For further knowledge on the subject I am indebted to the lad who took a liking for a pharmacist's diary he found lying around in Singapore and which contained up to date data on the subject of vitamins, although it was not the current issue.

From this diary I learned that vitamin B (either in the form of B1 or B2) was 'water soluble' – if that is worth anything. Nearby was a list showing the vitamins present in various eatables.

I don't suppose you knew, Ernest, that the yolk of an ordinary hen's egg was rich in Vitamin D, did you? Nor that it was a good source of vitamins A, B1 and E. Nor, I venture to think, did you know that white flour, such as finds its way into our delightful white bread (something I have only had in my dreams lately) contains no vitamins whatever – neither did I until I met that diary.

My interest being aroused I copied out all the details on the subject for my own benefit, and I don't mind telling you, I had many an eye opener. Take lettuce for instance. Its calorific value is only 2.8, but in spite of this it is a rich source of vitamins C and E. It is also a good source of vitamins A and B1, while B2 is also present, if the book is to be believed. Compare this with butter which has a calorific value of 225 (the highest on my list); or with beans with a calorific value of 100, while it only contains vitamin B1.

Another good one is milk, which, if my memory serves me well, was advertised extensively before the war as having a D some where in it. If it is vitamins they refer to then they should spell it with an A, B1, B2, C, D, E; for it contains the lot – B2 in good quantities.

But what is the good of talking of things I cannot get? Originally, I believe I was telling you how it all came about. However, once the theme was started we exchanged our field marshal's batons which were getting rather threadbare for the doctor's forceps, and talked 'dietetics'.

'Scrotum trouble' (I leave you to look it up in the dictionary the same as I did) originally blamed on lack of fats, now became blamed on the ever elusive vitamin B. The merits of 'unpolished' rice were enumerated, and the English housewife's custom of washing the rice was severely censured. 'Wash the rice and bang go your vitamins, if any,' was accepted among us as if it had been Boyle's Law among scientists.

We became rice critics, too, for that comes within the pale of dietetics. I told you a little about the different kinds of rice we have in a previous letter. If we are to believe those who claim to know more about the subject than I do, there are at least a dozen different kinds of rice. In most conversations on the subject I can hold my own I feel, as my neighbours are no better off than I am – they know nothing about it either!

Polished rice, unpolished rice, white rice, seed rice, parboiled rice, limed rice, broken rice and ground rice are enough to go on with in any conversation, while Japanese rice, Javanese rice, Siamese Rice and Burmese rice are worth talking about too. It's surprising what you can make up when you know nothing about it! We praised, slandered, condemned or compared rice with surprisingly vivid imaginations. We even grew sick of it. Then by way of variety we went into gruesome details of the precise deaths our respective beloved wives, mothers, cooks and housekeepers were going to suffer if ever they dared to serve up rice pudding when we got home.

Not only did we criticise the rice. We sat in judgement on each new dish that came along to help the rice down. It is not surprising that we differed in our opinions, I suppose.

For instance, when an extra brown queer tasting and rather gritty rissole appeared under the name of peanut meal rissole, we had to choose whether or not it was desirable. It's all very well to say that peanuts contain the jolly old vit B in plentiful quantities, but one must remember that peanut meal is marketed as a fertiliser for the benefit of farmers! Those who were anxious to collect the vitamins ate them, but those who were more particular and did not like the rather unpleasant and distinct 'bite' in the flavour, gave or threw them away.

On the matter of vegetables we are very vague. How can you be anything else when the cooks are found helping themselves to leaves from the hedges round about the place to cook for our 'greens'? We have some gardens though, and I am glad to say they are coming on fine, and some units have already sampled their produce. Not being a gardener I'm afraid I cannot tell you what is growing there apart from cucumbers and tapioca, but whatever it is makes a brave show and is 'coming on well'.

With all this talk however, we are no nearer solving the problem of 'what is a vitamin?' I peeped in a big medical book the other day and saw the latest chemical formulae for them – they seem to run a good second to our dear old friend of the school textbook, chlorophyll. I think they must be very unstable as they are very quickly destroyed if you muck about with them. One very respectable school of thought contends that if you boil, fry, roast, or tin vitamins, you destroy them. The question 'Does tinning fish destroy the vitamins?' has produced the hottest arguments without producing a satisfactory answer. We know the original fish had a goodly supply, but has it still got them when we open the tin?

If you find the answer, please let me know because I don't know who to believe, and it would be grand to quote a real authority on the subject.
Love to all
Alan

Chapter Seven

The Discovery of Talent

Roberts Hospital, 12 June 1942

My dear Ernest,

Four months have passed since we became prisoners of war, and as you may well expect, things have settled down considerably – especially in Roberts Hospital. Chaos has given way to order, and with it has come more time for leisure. As a schoolmaster Ernest, you will appreciate that to leave leisure hanging on folks hands is courting trouble, the folks concerned either get up to unthinkable mischief, or else go as rusty as a half-buried anchor whose only company is a cluster of barnacles and a wisp of seaweed.

Fortunately, we have had some chaps in our midst with sufficient energy and courage to start things moving.

One padre has gathered round him sufficient talent to throw a concert every fortnight. It started as an open air informal sing song, but now they use the old Changi cinema and call themselves the Red Cross concert party. Their fortnightly performances get a large audience in spite of lighting difficulties, and receive the appreciation they deserve.

Over in the dysentery wing, where I live, we have also been organising our own concerts, although on a much smaller scale – in fact I have even sung at them myself.

Believe it or not, Ernest, I sing comic songs that I have composed to fit well-known tunes, introduced by a little badly read patter in front of the 'microphone'. We are supposed to be broadcasting. Let me give you an example of what I sang, by a coincidence, on Empire Day. I tried to remember the words of Gilbert and Sullivan's 'When Britain really ruled the waves'. I managed the first two verses but failed on the third. Determined to have a third, I made it up myself as follows:

> When Cunnigham thrashed Italy
> Off dark Cape Matapan
> The high command at Singapore
> As you know well, ignored the War
> That threatened with Japan!
> Yet Britain still shall rule the waves
> In Good King George's glorious days!

It got a very good reception.

Men of a literary turn of mind have produced magazines. The 196 Field Ambulance (near neighbours of mine) produced a really good one, although it was really more for their own entertainment than for the whole area. More ambitious, was *Camp Pie*, produced by 32nd Company, which was circulated round the hospital. Having a larger field of talent to draw upon, it was bigger and better than the other. I hope that copies of these mags will be preserved so that the folk at home can be shown what we poor soldiers can do when we put our minds to it.

Other men, possessing organisational abilities, have entertained us with spelling bees, quizzes, debates and lectures to such an extent that we need hardly have a dull evening.

Perhaps we owe our good fortune in this respect to the fact that the hospital is composed of three distinct parts, run almost entirely independently of each other. There is 'Roberts' which is run by 32nd Company; 'dysentery wing' comprising the three Field Ambulances; and the AGH or Australian General Hospital. I think those men from all three parts, who have displayed such enterprise in the face of such difficulties deserve more praise than I can hope to give them in this letter. I have seen how they receive discouragement and no support from every side. They carry on, however, and put across whatever they are doing, and then others are sorry they did not try to help with this thing which has turned out such a success.

It was something like this that happened with the dysentery wing drawing competition.

One day early in May someone with plenty of enthusiasm and a heaven sent piece of chalk, wrote on our bungalow wall words to the effect that the closing date for entries was 25th May. Further information, gleaned from a paper circulated on the subject, showed that pencil sketches could be submitted under three headings (1) landscape, (2) still life, (3) poster.

I was still on the dhobi party and as the work was well in hand now and there was frequently very little for me to do, being an NCO, I conceived the idea of sketching our dhobi place and entering it in the competition. I had risen to the dizzy heights of NCO in charge under the officer who took us down to the sea, and as such I had been told that I was not expected to do the actual washing. This gave me plenty of time to do my sketching, as well as having a good swim with the lads when they had finished their work.

The dhobi place is a grand spot for an artist to use as a subject, and I felt even I would have a job to make a mess of it. I found a piece of shiny white Essex boarding which made an excellent little sketching block. It took me quite a long time, with plenty of rubbing out, but I enjoyed it. When I finally finished it I enlarged the picture on a piece of paper and carefully shaded it in. I was pleased with the result, and I hope that one day I shall be able to show it to you.

At the same time a brilliant idea struck me for a poster subject, which had to be based on a well-known slogan. No doubt, you will remember that all over the railway stations at home before I left could be seen the slogan 'It's quicker by Rail' and it struck me that this would give ample scope for sarcastic bathos.

I believe I told you of the limed rice, we had dished up. How at first we thought the cooks had mixed powdered egg preparation with the rice, and how besides smelling and tasting horrible it tarnished our spoons. I had grown to detest it as much as anyone. Nearly all of us avoided it like the plague, and whenever it appeared on the board you could be certain of a rapid crescendo to treble fortissimo in the murmurings and grumblings of the lads.

One cannot blame the cooks for dishing the stuff up. The Nips issued it for use, and we would grumble if the ration of good rice was small. They threw more into the swill pit than ever they served into the clamouring mess tins. The poor cooks could *not* get rid of the wretched stuff.

Therein lay the irony of my poster. I took as my full slogan: 'If it doesn't go fast enough, SEND IT BY RAIL, it's quicker!' 'It' was illustrated by three or four sacks of limed rice, while to illustrate the new speed attained by rail travel was a picture taken from true life on the dhobi gang, showing a few fellows pushing a wagon along the line.

I sent in my entries, and then followed a period of waiting in which all I could learn was that about a score of entries had been received altogether.

Being me, of course, I could not rest at one competition. 'Roberts' were advertising an exhibition in which anything from drawings to tin can models were to be shown. My wood carvings were nearly finished, so I set to with my jack knife and renewed vigour to make them presentable while I was waiting for the results of the drawing competition to be announced.

In case you don't remember, my wood carvings consisted of a nameplate for the front gate with 'Almea' on it, and a text to go on the wall, done in simple block lettering. I have chosen the text 'HE careth for YOU', from I Peter 5:7. As I chip and cut the fellows come and read the words and make comments. Many think them most inappropriate, but I find a great comfort in them. I wish they did.

I managed to finish the text, but I had to leave the name plate unfinished. Still, I put them both in and looked forward with trepidation to seeing them on show on the viewing day in two days' time.

By the way, I wish I could show you my jack knife that I use for carving. The marlinespike had been made into a little blade by patiently rubbing it on a piece of carborundum while I made a small chisel out of the broken tin opener.

View day came. What a show that was! It was held in the cinema, and as I walked in the first things I saw were my own carvings. Bashfully I turned my back, in case anyone should see my embarrassment, and immediately wished I hadn't. There on the wall were some of the best pencil sketches of still life I have seen. Temptingly displayed was a pile of fruit such as I have not seen for many a long day, while at its side was an open full cigarette case with the invitation to take one. The day was Wednesday and as the next issue of cigarettes would not be up till Thursday evening I guessed there were many feeling mad that they could not accept the gift. A cool glass of 'pop' sparklingly advertising its coolness and capability of satisfying, together with an ice cream that made me feel hot and thirsty.

Unlike the drawing competition, this exhibition had been well supported and there was an encouragingly large number of exhibits in every group. I was pleased to see efforts by the patients in the hospital, although some of them were copied from books, or showed a hand not skilled in wielding a pencil.

At last I had to focus my attention on the centre tables where the models and carvings were displayed. Closer inspection showed that my efforts sat quite comfortably in their surroundings. They did not 'let the side down' so I breathed more freely and looked at the prize winners.

First prize went to a length of bamboo about four inches in diameter on which had been carved a pattern such as one would expect to see on a cut glass vase. It was a marvellous piece of work and I hope the owner will be able to get it home safely when we are released, for it is worth keeping.

Second and third prize winners were also very good, and much better than mine. The things displayed – plaques, sculptured figures, aeroplane models, carvings – showed a standard of workmanship that amazed me. I wish you could have seen this exhibition for it was a revelation of resourcefulness when you remember the materials and tools with which we had to be content.

Two days after this, the results of the drawing competition came out, and to my utter amazement fellows started congratulating me on winning first prize!

I hurried off to where the sketches were on show, giving myself a mental pat on the back for my witty way of illustrating my slogan.

There was a surprise waiting for me, however, for the poster had drawn a blank. It was my landscape of the Dhobi Place which had received the award, although I considered there was at least one that was better.

All this makes you reflect, doesn't it Ernest? A column of soldiers in the street, uniform in their Khaki battle dress, and one thinks of them as nothing but soldiers, paid to kill or be killed and to be praised and honoured which ever way they go; and yet who can tell what talent is concealed beneath that khaki coat? I had to become a POW before I fully realised that they are not 'just soldiers', but may be actors, artists, sculptors, poets, writers, or organisers of no mean ability. Also I had to become a POW before I realised that I could lay claim to being an 'artist' and capable of producing with my own pencil things that might delight the eye.

They gave me ten cigarettes and a certificate for the first prize, and the joke of it is that the certificate was drawn in Indian ink by a real artist.

Love to all

Alan

'The Dhobi Place'
signed 'Walter', my nickname at the time

Chapter Eight

Lines of Communication

Roberts Hospital, 22 June 1942

My dear Ernest,
 At last we have written home – officially. That is an item of sufficient importance to keep us all talking for a month or so, I'm sure.
 Three days ago, after it got dark, we were all handed a postcard and told to write our message and hand it in again before 8 a.m. on the morrow.
 The postcard was a very interesting object. One side was left completely blank (obviously for the written matter to go on) and the reverse held an anaemic representation in orange of what was presumably the postage stamp along with a string of Japanese characters that did not interest us as we couldn't read them. There was space for a name and address.
 The 'stamp' – for such I insist on calling it – showed a fluffy tailed white dove perched on top of a Japanese war helmet and was enough to make anyone think. The incongruity of peace and war in such delightful relationship is apparent on first sight. I suppose it can be explained away by the hopeful and wishful thinking of the Nips who sincerely believe that through the trouble stirred up by their arms, a world peace will be established that will surpass

anything preceding it. Be that as it may, it was not for us to sit and admire the beauty or otherwise of our postcards as they appeared in the light of our oil lamps. Our job was to pay careful attention to the instructions given to us, and then concoct a written message saying everything we wanted to say in as few words as possible.

When you have not written a postcard for five months, it's a bit difficult, I assure you. Clearness of writing and meaning were required for we understood our captors were in no mood to waste time over bad writing, long epistles, or obscure meanings. No limits were set on the number of words so we had no means of telling whether we had written too much. It was worse than writing a telegram.

I found myself in the delightful position of doubting whether my own effort would be rejected or not as I had written about ten lines in block letters. I took the precaution of putting in a good word for the Japs as an added incentive for them to send it.

Anyhow, whatever the Nips thought about my postcard they have sent it on the first part of its journey. The letters have left the camp and to our knowledge they have reached Singapore. There they are waiting to be put on a boat.

I suppose you are wondering why I keep calling our captors Nips instead of always referring to them as Japs. Jap, as you know, is short for Japanese. Apparently some of these people insist that the real name of their land is Nippon and not Japan. They rather fancy themselves being called Nipponese. Don't ask me why. If it pleases them I don't mind, for it suits me. I rather fancy calling them Nips myself. After all, they all seem to be such little fellows.

All that is left for us to do now is to argue over the route our letters will travel: whether they will go via Portuguese Africa or Japan and across Russia. Perhaps they will go through Switzerland. When we are tired of that we can turn to arguing over how long they will take to reach home.

To argue and wait with patience for the day when we shall follow our letters.
Love to all
Alan

Chapter Nine

The Red Cross

Roberts Hospital, 14 July 1942

My dear Ernest,

You would be surprised how much our thoughts are taken up with the Red Cross. I must confess that before I became a POW I never gave much thought to this noble organisation. In fact, I've always done my best to steer clear of it until now. After all, you only go to see the doctor when you fear there is something wrong with you – or when you feel you can persuade the medical officer that you are not fit enough to do some unpleasant fatigues. When you are on the battlefield you always associate the Red Cross with unpleasant things like having your head blown off. You don't wonder that I've not been very thoughtful about it, do you Ernest?

All this changed when I became a POW. We talked and argued about it for months. We spoke in hopeful vein of its activities, giving particular attention to its work on behalf of the poor and needy in POW camps. We cited real and imaginary instances from the last war, and also this present one, to support our argument, and felt righteously indignant when anyone tactlessly told us that we did not know what we were talking about. Later we changed to contradicting each other over what the Red Cross was actually doing about us, and to theorising about the how, when, why and where it was going to make itself apparent.

It became quite the practice to burst into the hut and say 'Two Red Cross ships have come in!' and then when everybody looked up to add some witty remark such as 'But not in Singapore'.

No ship could be sighted off shore without it being claimed that it belonged to the Red Cross, even though it looked suspiciously like a ship of war. (We can see a fair bit of water from the roofs of the buildings in Roberts.)

Some even took to saying 'And Red Cross ships in the Harbour' or some such phrase to anybody telling a rumour that took more than a little swallowing, clearly implying that they had no intention of believing it.

But the Red Cross ships came in the end. Rumour gave way to fact and we saw, handled, and tasted ourselves. At last we have seen a little of what the Red Cross organisation can do. Thanks largely to them, we find it almost impossible to remember the food situation of three or four months ago.

And as only to be expected, we grumbled!

A list was posted up showing what foodstuffs had been issued to us. It made a brave show with nearly a score of different items. We were asked to vote on how it should be issued – whether it should be given to the cooks to pep up the meals (the officers were all for that) or whether we should have it issued straight to us. You can be sure we were unanimous in asking for all we could, for we reasoned that by putting the stuff in our hands we would know that we actually received it.

Several things like 'Maybela' porridge, some sort of flour, and dried vegetables were obviously cookhouse votes, but we wanted the jam and the sugar for ourselves – also the bully and the biscuits.

We got the jam in the end – a two pound tin between two – and I received (and tasted for the first time) that rather doubtful sounding, but very delicious jam labelled 'Tomato'.

One poor lad worried incessantly because he might get marmalade, which he could not eat. We told him that if he worried so much, he would get it. He did! Fortunately he was able to swap it with someone else.

We were given our sugar and biscuits, and also some special vitamised caramels (the delight of our hearts you may guess), but the bully and milk went to the cookhouse; and so we grumbled like true soldiers and were anything but content with our share.

You must not run away with the idea that food was all that came. The Red Cross also brought us a lot of needed medical supplies which went straight into the hospital and about which I know nothing. Maybe there were other things, but as far as we were concerned the food was the most important thing. That, above all else, filled our minds and our conversation.

Love to all

Alan

Chapter Ten

In Quest of Knowledge

Roberts Hospital, 3 August 1942

My dear Ernest,
 Ist der Sommer warm? Ja, er ist sehr warm. Ist der Winter kalt? Nein, er ist sehr warm auch!
 It's quite all right old boy, I've not turned pro-Nazi because I've been living under the old 'fried egg' lately. ('Fried egg' is our pet name for the Japanese flag, and a particularly apt description it is too, as you would agree if you saw the strong orangey yolks that seem common to the eggs out here.) I'm not even rehearsing my speech to darling Adolf on the climatic conditions of Singapore – or perhaps elsewhere.
 The fact is I'm endeavouring to learn a little German while I have the opportunity. I've always felt that a smattering of this language is helpful if you don't want to appear the complete ass, while it is useful when I come across odd snatches of German in any book I happen to be reading. We have an able teacher in our midst, and you will be surprised to hear that I'm enjoying it, a thing I never did when it came to learning French at school.
 German is not the only language being taught. French lessons are being given and a course in Russian is being arranged.

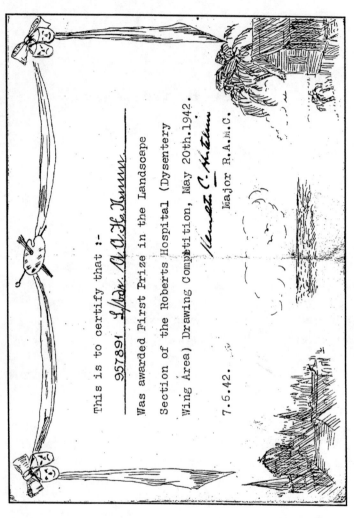

Certificate for First Prize

In the 18th Division area they have started Changi University, at which I had hoped to take a course in Economics had I not been sent to work in the hospital. I understand that a Secondary School has also been started for those who do not aspire to 'Universal Heights'.

The men who worked hard to get these seats of learning started deserve the highest praise, and certainly more success than they have enjoyed. The difficulties arising from working parties going to Singapore have sadly curtailed their efforts; and the students themselves have not been able to work under anything like decent conditions. I think very few men were able to complete the whole three months of the first term.

The quest for knowledge, however, is not easily thwarted. There are many around me here who have seized on text books and are seeking to turn otherwise barren months to some sort of profit, however small. Across the room a fellow has a book on company law – he hopes to be an accountant. Another fellow is teaching his neighbour mathematics. On every hand I find a thirst for learning, and even I have been approached and asked whether I could give a chap lessons in French, Mathematics, etc. Imagine me teaching French – what would Wee Willie say?

For myself, in addition to my German, I am trying to extend my acquaintance with literature, both modern and classical. It's a field I've seriously neglected in the past, and I am glad to find some really helpful books available. Dickens, Scott, R.L.S., Thackeray and George Eliot have been made to rub shoulders with H.G. Wells, Compton Mackenzie, Beverly Nichols and Howard Spring; and I do not believe that they or I have suffered for it.

Another profitable study has been the New Testament, which never fails to produce something new – some new conception or deeper meaning which sometimes rather astonishes me because I have not noticed it before. For surprising reading I recommend the Bible, especially when you read it with the hope of gleaning knowledge, and broadening your field or learning.

The quest does not end with the light of day. There are many, myself included, who delight to clamber, when we have the opportunity, up on the roof of one of the buildings and watch the sun set in all its blaze of tropical splendour, turning our eyes, ever and anon to the landscape around that grows mistier and dimmer in the failing light. On three sides we can see water. To the south, the sea – the open sea with nothing to break its surface till it weds the sky in a union that becomes more perfect as the sun declines, till at last we cannot tell the point of separation: – the sea and the way to freedom. Towards the sun, the channel up to the naval base stretches away from us, reflecting a thousand glories from the fiery sky, laying a burnished base to the most perfect painting it has ever been man's lot to witness – a painting always changing so that one is forced to gasp anew at every phase. In the foreground a few palms rear up in sombre silhouette to complete the delightful scene. We sit spellbound and speechless as the shades creep closer and the glory fades to a gentle tinting that reminds us, rather sadly, of what we have just seen. The twinkle of beacon lights dances across the water as if to show their triumph over their heavenly monarch in whose stead they must shine until he rises from his couch of rest with the return of day.

At last our tongues are loosened and I turn to Eddie with my almost nightly exclamation that the artist who paints sunsets is perfectly correct – even in his most lurid moments.

My friend voices his annoyance at my repetition and we fall to talking about 'bell ringing', or the scenery around our respective home towns.

Another night we would both listen to how 'Nobbie' struggled to success in his own business, his cockney accent ringing pleasantly in our ears with the words of wisdom.

And so we go on – ever seeking that which will broaden our minds and expand our knowledge because we are prevented by a line of barbed wire, a hostile army, and a world at war from living the lives we would wish to live, and from learning in the world of experience to provide for ourselves in the way we should most desire, or for which we consider ourselves most suited.

Love to all
Alan

PS

14 August. For once I am glad I've not been able to dispatch this letter, as last night a wonderful thing happened. The electric light came on! Not your carefully shaded, downwards only, black out lamps, but real bold brave lighting that streamed through the windows with peacetime gaiety. No blackout curtains and no fearful wondering if a chink of light was visible from without. It was wonderful! We walked round the hospital area and drank it in thankfully.

The reason for this peace-like innovation was to show would be attackers that we were under the protection of the Red Cross. A few days ago we had looked across at Changi jail (where the civilian prisoners had been herded) and seen the lights shining there.

I couldn't help thinking how queer the war was. Here was I, a miserable prisoner enjoying this peacetime sight while you, back home in England still furtively hide your light under a bushel. Funny, isn't it?

Chapter Eleven
Selarang

Roberts Hospital, 10 September 1942

My dear Ernest,

At the time when it happened we didn't know definitely what it was all in aid of. A party of lads from the hospital were detailed to be ready to move in two hours time with all their kit – dinner would be taken early so that the meal did not interfere with arrangements. At 5.10 p.m., forty minutes before zero hour, the sergeant came into the hut calling my name.

I stopped helping a chum to pack and turned about.

'Get your dinner at once – you're on this move.' Some unthinking ass had dropped out at the crucial moment. 'You'll have to hurry,' he added unnecessarily.

As if I didn't know! It would mean golloping my food at express speed with dire risk of indigestion, choking, hiccoughing, and insomnia later tonight, followed by a frantic bundling of all my worldly possessions into a kitbag and haversack hopelessly inadequate for the occasion. And I was right!

It meant more than that, for I had never attempted to pack my kit for hitting the trail since it had assumed the present proportions.

It seemed very little on paper, but it was surprising just how much kit I had.

Yes, Ernest, you are quite right – I did keep them waiting on the parade ground. For five minutes sundry sergeants and sergeant-majors (acting or otherwise) bawled out my name at the top of their respective voices. Not that I worried. After all, how could I be expected to arrive at the post with the others when I had given them a good hour's start?

Away we went with many a gibe and jest. We knew now that we were bound for Selarang – a block of barrack buildings across the valley about a mile away, some of which showed their blackened upper stories above the trees. They must have looked cool and imposing before the war came and painted them with tar to hide them from the eyes of Japanese pilots. We still wondered what it was all in aid of. Rumour stated, confirmed, contradicted, convinced and confused so rapidly that we were none the wiser, although in possession of many excellent and plausible theories.

All day, men had been streaming through the Hospital area on their way to Selarang from the 18th Div. and Southern areas with all their kit.

If you could have stood on the corner by the cinema (as I had done on several occasions earlier in the day) you would have been forced to smile and take your hat off to the ingenuity of the British soldier. As handcart after handcart passed one was reminded of the 'Streets of Adventure' gala day in aid of hospitals at home, and one wondered if there was to be a prize – not for the best decorated lorry or milk cart, but for the engineless lorry converted from its original use to the best hauled baggage carrier. One after another they had come, piled high with kit, food, chairs, tables, beds and every other conceivable comfort for such a hard, comfortless life.

To stand and watch that endless procession was also a revelation – of the ruthlessness of the conqueror, the subjection of the prisoners to his tyranny, the inexhaustible capacity of the British for adapting themselves to circumstances forced upon their shoulders, and above all, of the unconquerable spirit that will fling a jest into the face of fate when knees are sagging and backs are breaking under heavy loads. Here was heartlessness. Here also were ingenuity and cheerfulness, not unseasoned with a sense of humour which asked to break out on the slightest provocation!

Our contingent had its own quota of baggage wagons, and as we were all so heavily laden with our personal kits, a fatigue party was laid on to supply the motive power. When it came to the time for the fatigue party to return to the hospital the Japs refused to let them go. They had to stay with us. All their kit left behind, wanted, but unpacked, untidy, unobtainable, and useless to them at the moment.

As we journeyed from our area, down our side of the valley, then up the other side and into the other area, I reflected on the difference between my present mode of transport and that of the Aussie ration party that passed regularly over the same route. They did the journey in about a fiftieth of the time, and we used to love the thrill of watching them do it. They would bring their wagon (an adapted lorry) to the top of the far slope, receive the 'okay' from the Sikh sentry, pile aboard and then let her rip. The wagon would hurtle down the hill gathering enough momentum to carry it across the flat and up our slope and (if it was a good run) into our gate. The return run was just as thrilling, but as the far slope was higher than our side, they usually stopped a good few yards short of the gate, and we could see the men hurriedly jump off and push until the wagon was out of sight.

We were among the last to arrive. Having parked my kit on an available square inch of grass I looked around. What a sight! Try to imagine a barrack square bounded on three sides by six tall rectangular black blots which were once palatial building of true military uniformity rendered in white, cool looking concrete, but now obliterated externally by a coat of tar (or creosote) in honour of the recent war, yet still showing patches of whiteness from interior surfaces, and reminding one of a rough watercolour in which the artist has not bothered to make his different colours meet. Try to imagine, too, a photograph of Blackpool, Brighton, and Southend combined on an August bank holiday, superimposed upon it and you might have some idea of what the scene was like. It was not as bad as the Black Hole of Calcutta, I admit; we were not as tightly packed as those poor chaps on the *Altmark*, but it was infinitely more impressive. The crowd in the square did credit to Mitcham Fair on a record breaking day and the buildings literally bristled with men, as tightly packed as flies who have found a fish of decided antiquity lying on the pavement in the height of summer. Perhaps you would see it better if I compared it with one of those inverted flower pots in the garden at home covering an ants' nest, from which we have taken the stone covering the hole, and into which we have stuck a stick to stir up the ants. Do you remember how they used to come pouring out and go helter-skelter in all directions till no part of the flower pot could be touched with the finger without annihilating at least one of them? If that doesn't convey a sufficient impression, think of a length of fly paper such as can be seen in cheap city eating houses and which has been left up a week or so till you wonder whether its capacity is full and its period of usefulness over. If you have the picture in mind with men in place of ants or flies, then you have some idea of Selarang. There was very little for me to do. Fatigue parties had already been laid on from the other units and there was no shortage of labour. Foremost among the tasks was the digging of latrine trenches in the asphalted parade ground. These trenches were fifteen feet deep and thirty feet long, and dug through very hard stony ground with only picks and shovels.

Out in the open, where I was parked, we found the sun very hot, so we rigged up a cover with groundsheets and gas capes. Under this we crouched and I read my book. Later I joined three friends and was initiated into the mysteries of playing bridge. This was certainly one way of passing the time even if not the most perfect. (As a novice at the game I'm afraid I trumped my partner's ace on at least one occasion.)

We couldn't take much exercise. As far as I could judge we were confined in an area about three hundred by two hundred yards. In this area the Japs had poured seventeen thousand prisoners.

I went to visit the lads from my old unit whom I had not seen since I went into the hospital. I found them jammed into one of the barrack blocks and quite cheerful. I also found they were near the boundary of our prison area. There was no wire, no bars, no fence! Just an order that we were not to step on the road. I saw some wicked looking Japs with machine guns at the ready and decided I did not like the look of them. I threaded my way back to my bivouac, my book, and my bridge.

I heard singing, and from my shelter I looked towards the tall smudgy barrack buildings. A concert was in progress. A stage had been raised about level with the heads of bystanders and on this some sort of performance was proceeding. The singing was caught up by several thousand voices, and I wondered what the Japs thought. These mad English! No wonder the Japs don't understand us.

A fellow took the stage dressed in white and trying to look like a girl. I couldn't see very well what he was doing but it seemed some sort of burlesque of a strip tease act. Very vulgar, no doubt, but it raised laughter from the bristling buildings as well as from hundreds of 'groundlings' standing round the built-up stage.

By this time we knew why we were being squeezed together like this. The Japanese High Command in Tokyo had told the local commander that we were to sign papers promising to make no attempt to escape. This paper also pointed out that men who broke this promise would be liable to be shot on recapture.

Such a procedure is entirely contrary to international law. I've not read the law on the subject but from what I've been told it is recognised as a soldier's duty to try and escape should he ever be captured. He risks court martial after the war if he doesn't. Another point about escaping is that a man is not to be condemned to death merely because he escaped – killed while resisting recapture, if you like, or executed for murdering somebody in the course of escape, but not death as a punishment for escaping.

All this had been explained to us by our officers, with the result that we all refused to sign.

Frustration in the Japanese local command! No doubt hara-kiri would have to be committed by the unworthy local command if gracious orders of the excellent high command were not carried out.

The prisoners had to be made to sign. How? 'Put them all in a concentrated area and keep them there without supplies until they sign.' We took our own supplies with us and two full days passed.

'Move the patients out of Roberts Hospital into Selarang area.' That did the trick. We could not allow anything so inhumane. Dysentery had already broken out among us as it was.

Our officers ordered us to sign, explaining that the emphasis was on the 'ordered'. That put the blame on the officers and would let us out in any court martial proceedings. The whole thing was done under duress so we could consider ourselves not bound by our signatures.

Next day, 5 September, we packed up our belongings and trooped back to our respective areas. I found myself back again in Roberts Hospital, thankful that the affair was over, and anxious to know what Old Man Rumour had to say about it all.

That old friend, or arch enemy (whichever you choose to call him) had been very busy. There is no point in telling everything we heard for much was rapidly revealed to be untrue. The straightforward story is that Selarang was the result of our refusal to sign those papers. There was something else however. We all feel convinced that the dastardly execution of four soldiers the first day of Selarang is bound up with this somewhere. Let me tell you about it.

A few days before Selarang happened, Captain Philips RAMC and a party were lawfully proceeding from one area to another when they were stopped by guards. The captain, two sergeants and an Eurasian lad were picked out and taken away, accused of having tried to escape. They were condemned to be shot. Only the intervention of our highest officers prevented this taking place in front of the seventeen thousand of us crammed into Selarang.

If the execution had taken place at Selarang nobody doubts but that some of our men, losing their self-control, would have tried to interfere. The Japs would have been ready with their machine guns trained on us. Hundreds would have been killed in the ensuing 'riot', an incident that no doubt could have been twisted into propaganda somehow. Mercifully, the execution finally took place on the sea shore. Some of our high-ranking officers were compelled to be present. It was a gruesome affair as the Sikh firing squad seemed curious to find out how many bullets they could put into the victims before they killed them. The poor men died like heroes.

That is the story and I believe there is a lot of truth in it, although I am at a loss to understand why the Japs should want to create such an incident.

Selarang is over however. Whether it will find its way into popular history only time can tell. It was not nearly as bad as the Black Hole of Calcutta. The conditions on the *Altmark* were far worse, although comparatively a handful of men suffered. Surely seventeen thousand men must carve a niche somewhere. Perhaps it will be in the dictionary where I discovered Maffeking. Who knows, in a few years' time people doing the London sales will be saying, 'My dear, there was a perfect Selarang in the Department. I literally had to fight my way out after getting that hat!'? Perhaps doctors will use the word in connection with an emergency operation for appendicitis. Rumour has it that one took place while we were there.

Love to all

Alan

Chapter Twelve
Change of Address

Chungkai, Thailand, 18 November 1942

My dear Ernest,

You will notice that I have changed my address. Not that I particularly wanted to, but there was nothing I could do about it. A party was detailed from the hospital to reinforce the medical staff in Siam, and yours truly was included – not because of any superior medical knowledge or surgical skill, but because I had two legs that worked and could carry things.

The journey up was really a terrible night- (and day) mare. We were bounced down to Singapore station by lorry and packed aboard a train. The railway lines are narrower than standard gauge and that gave the whole place a slightly ridiculous look. I was not surprised to find that there were no passenger carriages for us to travel in – after all, even in France you expect cattle trucks: '8 chevaux (en long) 40 hommes' sort of thing. There were no cattle trucks however, and we packed into wagons originally intended for transporting partly processed rubber. They were made of metal and (like the French cattle trucks) had a sliding door in the middle of each side. The size of each truck according to my calculations was seventeen feet long, seven feet wide, and seven feet high. Into one of these about thirty of us were jammed. Life was further complicated by the lumpy mattress of sacks of rice on which we tried to settle ourselves. I suppose we were lucky – some had hard wooden boxes of stores to contend with.

The journey lasted five days and proved utter misery. During the day the sun beat down on the metal roof nearly roasting us alive, and making us long for the night. If this heat was relieved by a rain storm, the doors had to be practically closed to keep us from getting drenched, and then we had no air. When day gave place to night the roasting heat gave place to cold, and condensation was so heavy on the walls that they streamed with moisture. What with this, and the noise, and not being able to see whose foot was being put in your mouth, or whose side you were poking with your knee, we just longed for the morning. And of course our tempers got worse as we went along.

We passed through Kuala Lumpur. The railway station was roofed over and evidently meant to be imposing, but all efforts in this direction had only succeeded in making it look ridiculous. It seemed hard to believe that before the war there were more millionaires per square mile in KL than in most other places. It was the home of the rubber and tin kings.

And so on, through the length of Malaya, stopping at stations with names that sounded familiar because of the war that had raged here nearly a year before. We passed through Ipoh, the scene of very bitter fighting. The evidence of war was still around us and sometimes we would crawl timorously over temporary bridges thrown alongside the wrecks of useful looking iron bridges that had been destroyed when British troops had retreated. We crossed the border into Siam, or Thailand as it now appears to be called. Life became a little more interesting, if only because of the novelty of seeing different writing on the station signboards. The Siamese have a writing of their own, and it looks most intriguing.

Eventually, we were ordered from the train at a sizeable town called Bangpong. I was disappointed that we did not go another thirty miles for I believe that would have brought us to Bangkok, and I always get a thrill when visiting places I learnt about at school.

We stayed here a few days, living in native huts made of bamboo and palm leaves; and getting our first experience of bartering with the local inhabitants (although this latter was contrary to the wishes of the Japanese). I tried my hand and won two dollars for a broken fountain pen with an odd top. 'Pretty good for an amateur,' I thought.

From Bangpong we were taken by lorry about ten miles along quite a good road to another town on the banks of a river a little wider than the Thames at London. This was Kanjong-buri, and what an exciting place it was! First there was the high wall – a delightfully oriental pink in colour – that might have been a defence for the town. Then there were the streets of houses and shops, with here and there an imposing building that was obviously important. There was an open space and a real private car parked on it. Although there was dirt and poverty in places, the bright sunshine made the colours light and gay among the dark green riot of sub-tropical vegetation. To my eyes it looked a quaint and charming place with its primitive attempts at modern civilisation.

We were dumped near the river and herded together between some houses backing on to it to wait for boats. It was pleasant under the dense foliage of some trees, so we did not mind the long wait. I ate my haversack rations given me before we set out. The strangest, yet one of the best haversack rations I've ever had – a bunch of six bananas! Thailand is the home of bananas.

The boat came and we stowed aboard for the last leg of our journey. It was only about two miles, and seemed to lay up a tributary that joined the main river at Kanjong-buri.

We pulled into land and were helped ashore by men from the camp. Greetings were called and faces lit up when news of friends was forthcoming from either side.

Once ashore I was amazed to see that further progress was barred by a shallow sheet of water flooding the nearby buildings, including the cookhouse immediately in front of me.

We hesitated, but were not lost because the men from the camp splashed into the water and helped us ashore, showing us where to put our feet and holding our hands to help our balance. They seemed totally indifferent to getting their boots filled with water as long as we landed with dry feet. I hope I said thank you to them for it was a very decent thing for them to do.

This was Chungkai Camp, and for the first night we had to sleep in the open. I reflected on the stupidity that led people to build in such floodable places.

We were shown the huts we were to occupy and found them like the ones at Bangpong but longer, and with the far ends protruding out of four feet of flood water. The near ends were still crowded with anxious men wondering whether they would have to make a hurried (and damp) exit in the middle of the next night.

After a few days, the tide went down and we were able to take possession of our piece of hut. Things didn't stop there, however, for the tide fell still further until I found that the point where I had stepped ashore was more than twenty feet above the normal level of the river! I hastily withdrew certain thoughts on stupidity, thankful that I had not voiced them. Chungkai camp was really very sensibly placed, well above the river, which had been swollen by abnormally heavy rains up country when I arrived.

The hut in which I am living deserves description since it appears that such shelter is intended to be my home for the duration of our stay in Siam.

The sole materials needed are stout bamboo poles and palm leaves, and the simplest way to describe the finished article is to suggest that the builder was so absent minded as to forget all about the walls and start building the roof on the ground.

The lower end of the bamboo rafters rest on the ground, but as the palm leaf roofing does not start below five foot up the effect is reminiscent of a ridge tent of impossible length, with the brailings tightly rolled and the guy ropes unduly stout.

'Why are you in Siam?' I can hear you ask. I suppose it's a military secret really but the Japanese have decided that a railway would help the cause of progress – bring civilisation to the remotest corners of the land, etc., and being very kind people they consider it their duty to achieve this. After all, there is plenty of slave labour in the POW camps.

I cannot say I am pleased about the change. There is more food to eat, and we don't feel so closed in (although there is a bamboo fence round the camp) but somehow life seems much more uncertain than before and I find that very disturbing.

Love to all

Alan

Chapter Thirteen

Casual Labour

Chungkai, Thailand, 14 December 1942

My dear Ernest,

A fortnight ago I broke my association with the hospital – at least, they broke the connection for me, for I had no option in the matter. What apparently happened was that the Nips decided the hospital at Chungkai could function just as efficiently with a depleted staff, whereas their precious railway could not be built to schedule as efficiently without a little extra help.

So out into the cruel cold world of working parties I was sent to toil: out from the protective covering of the Red Cross – flimsy though it may be. Frankly, I'm disgusted about it all; not only does it mean that I'm thrown into much closer contact with our taskmasters, but that I am required to help their war effort by building this horrible railway. They tell us a lot of rot about development of interiors, progress, and other nice sounding ideas, but there is not one of us that cannot see they are far more concerned with getting men and materials up into Burma. Unfortunately (or is it fortunately?) I've only got my convictions on the subject. Maybe that's because the courage wouldn't do me or anyone else any good!

IMPERIAL JAPANESE ARMY

I am interned in No. 2 POW THAILAND
My health is ~~excellent~~. usual. ~~poor~~
~~I am ill in hospital.~~
I am working for pay.
~~I am not working~~
Please see that MOTHER'S CAT is taken care

My love to you
A. Alan H. Nunn

'The One that Got Away'
The only communication received by Eileen all the time I was a POW. 'Mother's Cat' gave those at home the clue I was in Siam. The cat was half Siamese.

Now that I am out of the hospital I realise just how desirable that Red Cross covering is. Although I was only an auxiliary who collected firewood and did not wear a Red Cross arm band, I took my orders from the doctors, and had practically nothing to do with the Nips. And the Nips have a habit of pushing you around!

Mind you, it's not always as bad as that. If you manage to keep your sense of humour it helps a tremendous amount, and you can get quite a few laughs at the Nips' expense – providing their backs are turned. And sometimes you may 'click' for a good job.

The other day, for instance, I was detailed to take charge of ten men going down river by barge to Kanjong-buri to pick up a motor car. It cannot be more than about four miles to Kanjong-buri, but the job took us all the morning. What a rare time we had getting that car on board! A real case of science as applied in the Far East.

We took with us on the barge a magnificent collection of timber of all shapes and sizes – double what we needed – together with a formidable array of tools from saws to toothpicks.

The task in hand was to rig up a ramp down which the car could be run on to a temporary deck we had to fix up for the purpose. The amazing thing was that by hook or crook we contrived to use all the timber we had brought. My one disappointment was that some of the tools defied all the ingenuity of the Nips to find jobs for them.

The same afternoon found us in another barge on our way down to Kanjong-buri to pick up another cargo. (I could make a good pun out of that, but I won't.) We never discovered what that cargo was, for after hanging about till past teatime we came back empty-holded.

The return journey found us with two weights on our minds. The first was wondering if the cooks had saved our supper for us, or whether it had gone the way of all rice. The second was planning the best way to keep in on a good job. There were many other jobs for such casual labourers as we, and some of them were best avoided. We knew there had been a technical hitch somewhere so we wondered just what could be done about it. We pumped the Nip in charge of us and won from him a request for our services on the morrow. On parade next morning we told the officer of this arrangement and gleefully made for the barge, full of hope for another pleasant day.

But there, Ernest, we sadly bit our fingers! Our cargo was waiting for us this time – it consisted of bales of rice sacks and bundles of large iron staples that were just too heavy to heave around in comfort. After tiffin it was a most unenthusiastic party that dropped down river for a repeat order, for we had had a very hard morning.

It never rains, but what it pours, as you know. On our return journey a truant gust of wind whipped off my Red Cross hat, and I had the mortification of seeing it picked up by some 'wogs' in a boat behind. I could have sold it to them for three dollars and that is a lot of money – about a month's pay.

Another job I got caught for on another occasion was 'jungle clearing'. Now I have heard all about these tropical jungles – their denseness, the prolific vegetation, their impenetrability (good word that!), and I wanted to see one for myself. The fact is I took such adjectives with rather a pinch of salt – especially the last one! Many times during the Malayan campaign, when our flanks were protected by impenetrable jungle, or impassable swamps, the Japs made their way through at that particular point and succeeded in turning those flanks – if the average soldier can be believed.

At first sight the Thai jungle disappointed me: a few tall trees with fronds hanging from their branches down to the ground and inviting one to play Tarzan and the Apes (with the Japs very appropriately taking the part of the apes) a few smaller trees and saplings such as one might expect to find in a good old English wood, and an odd clump or two of bamboo thrown in to remind you that you were in the tropics. Impenetrable jungle? Bah!

We set to work.

Half an hour's assault with parang and cockeyed saw on the nearest clump of bamboo, without any visible impression convinced me I had underestimated somewhere, and that a few dozen such clumps strategically sprinkled over the landscape could take the sting out of the most ferocious bayonet charge.

Bamboo has to be seen to be believed. No doubt it starts life as a respectable little shoot, starting up green and starchy from the rich earth. By the time man arrives, all intent on building a railway, the respectable shoot has married and produced an offspring worthy of a prize sow and remains there looking on while his grandchildren, great-grandchildren, great-great etc., etc., sprout up around his feet. The result is a clump twenty feet in diameter and sixty feet high to the tip of the tallest patriarch, and immensely prickly. When bamboo dies it does not lie down – it can't! Its descendants have not only closely crowded round him, but have stretched out their arms every foot or so to embrace all the relatives within reach. The interlacing and embracing that goes on forms a network of barbed points that would make barbed wire untangle itself in disgust.

I saw enough jungle before the day was out. It may not have been the densest obtainable, but it certainly satisfied my curiosity, and was quite jungly enough for me.

An amusing incident happened while we were jungle clearing. I hope I can make it sound as funny as it appeared to us.

The method of procedure is to attack a massive clump of bamboo with parang and saw (the teeth of which are set backwards so the cutting stroke is the pull instead of the push), and when every stalwart shoot has been sawn through, to hitch a rope round the lot and obey the Nip's command of 'All men pull'. After enough practice for a tug-of-war team the defeated clump is dragged aside to where it can be burned.

We had got to the pulling stage with a particularly obstinate clump, and were having a breather when our Nip foreman decided on a practical demonstration. He tugged and pulled without success for a while, and then enlisted the help of one of our lads with a small ginger beard and sailor-like hat set at a jaunty angle. We stood and watched while the Nip urged 'Sailor-hat' to pull – which he did with every display of effort but very little effect. Punctuating the grunts and urgings of the Nip, we heard the voice of 'Sailor-hat'. 'Me no good – you okay. You very good – me dummy dummy. You number one.'

We could see that with every word of praise the Nip pulled harder, till he was doing as much as six of us and nearly breaking a blood vessel. And the more he pulled, the less did 'Sailor-hat' pull until he was doing little more than holding the end of the rope. 'Me dummy dummy – me no good.' As far as the Japs are concerned, 'Sailor-hat' never said a truer word.

Jungle clearing is hard work, and it was with thankful hearts we shouldered our weapons and made for camp, leaving a pile of bamboo burning with flames roaring a hundred feet high.

I seem to have settled for a regular job now, and it's a grim one. Half a mile beyond the camp the river washes the base of a rocky spur without leaving room for a decent footpath – let alone a railroad. Here, a cutting is being blasted through the rock. First the drillers attack the cliff face with hammer and cold chisel, knocking holes a metre deep in the tough old stone. Charges are fixed and a Jap performs a jaunty little tune on his bugle while perched on a pinnacle of rock high above our heads. Everybody retires and 'Up she goes!'

Then I start work. Scrape and scratch, pull and prise, dig and drag. Large rocks, small rocks, rubble and dust. All the loosened rock must be cleared away. Heavy rocks and sharp rocks, rocks without end. Basket after basket of rubble passes from hand to hand down two long chains of men and is emptied into trucks and then goes careering down the two rickety switchback tracks to the emptying point. A few moments respite for those in the basket chains, and back they come for the next loads. Shovel, chunkle, rake, crowbar, pickaxe and hammer all clashing in a chorus of pandemonium which is caught by the rocky walls, magnified, and flung back again till one's head feels swollen and almost dizzy. And above all, the hot sun beats down, growing hotter as the day ages; beating down with noontide intensity on our bare backs, striking at us from the white rock with a glare that burns our eyes and forces us to crease our faces till our eyes are all but hidden.

Oh! the slowness with which the hours revolve! Oh! how welcome is the break for tea (no milk or sugar!) Oh!

how weary my legs grow towards evening, and oh! how thankful I am when we knock off! Where does the strength come from to get back to camp? I don't know. Back I would stagger under the unbelievable weight of a chunkle, and flinging it eagerly into a pile, make for my hut with scarcely any lighter step. I can't keep this up for long – really I can't. I shall die of fatigue in a week if I try. There is no respite unless I go sick – I'll have one day off then, at least. Yes, I shall go sick, and keep going sick, until I feel stronger. It's early yet, but I feel so tired – I must go to bed.
Love to all
Alan

Chapter Fourteen
Christmas 1942

Chungkai, Thailand, 28 December 1942

My dear Ernest,

'Christmas comes but once a year, and when it comes it brings good cheer!' It's an old saying Ernest, but there's any amount of truth in it.

Thanks to co-operation from the Nips we were able to have some 'good cheer' – even if it was a meagre ration. We couldn't do things in style, of course, out in the wilds of the 'Thaiamese' jungle with only the promise of a railway between us and the nearest civilisation.

Still, we had a holiday, special grub, entertainments and carols, which shows that someone tried to bring a little colour into our lives. Instead of the usual Saturday holiday we get, the Nips allowed us the Friday, certainly an encouraging start. Then they granted us a little extra meat and other sundries, along with three hundred dollars (among the six thousand in camp) to buy a few extras.

Messing committees got down to work, and two or three days before the 25th we had an imposing menu pinned on the notice-board. It was imposing because at first many of us had little idea what some of the items meant. 'Chungkai Rice' obtained its name from our place of encampment, but that didn't tell us it was mixed with vegetables, was rich in onions and had a definitely salty tang. 'Crochette' for breakfast did not refer to two quavers but to a rissole. However, we could understand fried egg, roast beef, and roast pork, also roast potatoes, peanuts, orange, banana, and lime. Sweet coffee and tea were also luxuries. We appreciated this rarity immensely, even if our stomachs suffered afterwards for our folly. When one thinks of Christmas pudding and turkey, not to mention mince pies and stuffing it may seem pretty lame, but to us it was a feast!

The entertainments were provided by a few enterprising individuals who probably had their own interests in mind and well to the forefront when exerting their energies. I'm sure it wasn't all prepared and produced after they came back from working parties. 'Rhythm on the River' was well advertised by attractive and artistic posters as 'A concert to be presented in the jungle theatre at 4 p.m. and 7.30 p.m. on Christmas Day'. I did not go myself, but heard that it was a commendable success and worth seeing. Some other lads organised dog-racing with wooden dogs on a large oval track complete with tote, touts, bookies and all the other accessories for betting. It was really a glorified game of Ludo and judging by the noise they made not far from my tent all the morning a good time was being had by all – except those who lost.

The hospital – steeped in isolation because of diphtheria – was treated to a few carols by the choir in the afternoon, the singers being rewarded afterwards by a cup of coffee.

Yes Ernest, you are quite right in thinking that I was in the choir. I stumbled on to a choir practice one night and realised that it was just what the doctor should have ordered. The practices were enjoyable and jolly; and even if the lighting was bad and we had difficulty in following our scores, we became moulded into some sort of shape and sallied forth on Christmas Eve to sing round the camp. The Salvation Army lads had been doing this for several days already, but we had some new ones to sing so could hardly be accused of copying. I really enjoyed it, for I could not lightly forget my last year's disappointment when after two or three weeks' practice we were unable to have our carol service on the boat coming out.

As I have said already, we sang to the hospital on Christmas afternoon, but the highlight of our career was last night's carol service in the church. We sang nice carols, only three of which were generally known. I like the new ones I learnt (or should I say the old ones I learnt) and have made a note of where I can find them for future reference. I was surprised to find how weak one's voice can go with lack of practice; I really had hard work to get through the tenor of some of the pieces. I shall have to do some systematic training when I come home!

There was plenty of singing about the camp during the evening; but as there was no drink about it lacked that intoxicated abandonment that one has learnt to associate with a soldier's carousal, and that slovenly slurry singing that seems so dear to his heart. One felt sure, nevertheless, that nobody was going to let Christmas pass without making an effort to introduce a little 'good cheer' to remember it by. And so the day drew to a close. 'Lights Out' blared out with unnecessarily blatant vigour considering it was Christmas; the singing grew softer and the voices sank to a murmur. One by one the flickering lamps were abruptly quenched, until one felt that the only sensible thing to do was to go to sleep.

Love to all

Alan

Chapter Fifteen
Ring Out! Ye Bells

Chungkai, Thailand, 1 January 1943

My dear Ernest,

In order to give 'the Jocks' a chance, I suppose, we had another holiday today instead of Saturday this week. Not that today's festivities are in any way as great as a week ago, but there is something about the air which suggests merrymaking. The grub has been pepped up a bit although very little extra was spent on it than on a normal day. The 'dogs' and the concert are booked for appearances later on this afternoon.

I feel that the best way I can celebrate the New Year is to write to tell you the situation as we see and understand it here.

To us, the advent of 1943 means but one thing – the last year of the war. We tell each other it will all be over, and that before the wheel of time completes another revolution we will be free. In fact, we are determined that 1943 will go down to history and posterity alike as the year in which the war ended. What we shall, or can do if it doesn't end, doesn't enter our heads. 'Hope springs Eternal in the human breast', to quote the poet, and we feel a surge of that peculiar property passing through us today.

Mind you, outward signs of the inward 'sentimentalities' are absent. At the time when all the bells of Thailand ought to have been hurrying out the old year, and heralding in the new, I, like most other people in the camp, had been sound asleep for an hour, not caring two figs whether they (the bells) shook themselves free of their moorings and came crashing down from the top of their respective belfries. Whether the Thais are addicted to this habit, I know not. It happens to correspond with their New Year as far as I can see, so it's on the cards that they are.

To them, however, it is not 1943. Oh no! Days and months may correspond numerically with ours, but the year has to be written thus:

พ.ศ. ๒๖๘๖

– which being interpreted is BE 2486! Heaven only knows what the BE that precedes the number of the year stands for.

But we look back over the year that has passed as everybody does, or says they do. 1942 will always stand for the year I spent in captivity, the year in which I was released from all the conventions of civilisation, and needed not heed the voices of 'correctness' and 'good taste'. It was the year in which I did not have to shave till the growth on my chin grew irritable; and could go to church in only a pair of underpants. Above all, perhaps, it was the year that was wasted and left a blank. No, not wasted or left a blank, for on looking back I see many an interesting episode connected with it. A year, rather, in which I marked time while a war raged and I grew older, speculating as I grew on how I would fit back into that little circle from which I had been so rudely snatched. A year in which news came to me only through the channel of rumour, or (when from authorised source) heavily leavened with exaggeration.

And what rumours they were! Nearly always cheerful, and so often repeated that we would fain believe them in spite of our incredulity. Never has a war finished so many times as that which raged at the beginning of this year, and which – to our surprise – still raged at its close. Nor have so many campaigns been successfully concluded so many times. Truth and falsehood slung at us side by side so that we are unable to distinguish the one from the other.

At the time of 'going to press', we know that the Libyan campaign is over and that the last German troops are being speedily mopped up. We are likewise certain that the Russians have advanced many miles and our foes are broken beyond effective rallying. We have heard for sure that General Wavell has started an offensive in Burmah. But how can we be sure that tomorrow will not prove it all wrong?

Wrong or right, however, it is on this we feed, and at the moment we are building ethereal castles on the strength of it. We shall be free soon, and then I shall not need to write to you; I shall be able to tell you all about my adventures. 'Ring out ye Bells!' as the poem says, 'Ring out the Old' and with it take our captivity. 'Ring in the New' – a newness that speaks of freedom!

Love to all

Alan

Extract from Original Manuscript
We were prisoners longer than we bargained for so we had to conserve paper.

Chapter Sixteen

Once I Built a Railroad

Tarsoh, Thailand, 24 April 1943

My dear Ernest,

Nearly four months have passed since I penned my last letter to you, and in all that time I have been unable to write a single line.

A lot has happened since then, and now I'm a bit hazy over my dates.

We finished work on the Chungkai quarries at the end of January; but not before a compressor had been brought up so that pneumatic drills could be used for drilling holes for the dynamite charges.

I had a hand in fixing that compressor in one position. It's a heavy machine and took a lot of pulling and pushing to shift it. When at last we had it in its new position we found we could not fix the first length of iron piping taking the compressed air to the drills, because of a wall of rock. The pipes were straight, and we needed a bent one to overcome our difficulty. What should we do? Being British workmen, we scratched our heads, looked helpless, and wondered from where the machine for bending pipes was coming.

Not so the Nips. The twin stumps of an overgrown bush (or undersized tree) provided them with an inspiration. Place the pipe between the stumps at the required point for bending and 'all men pull'. All men pulled lustily and the pipe bent without buckling or splitting. The compressor was able to do its work perfectly, as I found to my cost later, when back working on the quarries. The noise of these drills hammering away at the dazzling white rock face added greatly to our discomfort when with many others, I scraped and scratched, heaved and humped rock and rubble blasted down by the previous explosion.

When the quarries were finished, we received marching orders; and shouldering all our worldly belongings, we trekked up the course of the railway to our next sphere of labour.

I don't remember if I told you before, that other parties of slaves had been sent to camps further up-country than Chungkai, and while we were busy blasting cuttings, they had been making embankments, bridges, and more cuttings all along the line. When we moved from Chungkai we found a pretty level road for much of the way.

The camps dotted along the route were not very far apart really, although when weighed down with all your kit, you were only too thankful to reach the next one. I have a kit bag full of stuff, and in order to make carrying easier I have fixed some shoulder straps from a pack so that it rides high on my shoulders, which is the best place for a heavy load. That's a tip I've learnt in my travels Ernest: don't adjust your pack so that all the weight hangs half way down your back – get it as high up on your shoulders as possible.

To help the journey along, I tried to chart the course of the railway. I could only do it roughly, of course, but by noting the position of the sun and the time of day, I was able to get some sort of bearings. Distance could be judged by counting paces, which I did for quite a bit of the time. There's no doubt about it, Ernest, the old Scout training does come in useful.

We stopped for the first night at Wan Lung, which showed signs of previous civilisation in the shape of a tobacco plantation. The camp adjoined it, and consequently our men were in clover; for tobacco was cheap if you bought it, and easy to pick if you didn't. Some experimented with curing it, and even claimed tolerable success.

At this camp a platform had been achieved by banking up earth beside the track-to-be, and then marching the working parties up and down it for a couple of days until it was trodden firm. The comments made by our men both at the time, and when recounting the incident later, can be imagined.

The next day brought us to Wan Ti Kien, or One Tuck In as I prefer to call it, as it was a place where we got plenty of food. We stayed here and worked for a few weeks levelling up the railway track. I went down with dengue fever and spent a week in hospital. There was an advantage in this, because the hospital was in a hut lately occupied by Nips, and consequently better built than our sleeping quarters, and the bamboo slats were more comfortable to lie on.

From One Tuck In we moved to Bankau – about five kilometres, and did more embankment building.

I have never described embankment building to you, have I? Perhaps I had better do so, then you will have a clear picture in your mind of what I am supposed to be doing.

The tools required for the job consisted of pickaxes, chunkles, ordinary axes (in case your embankment happened to be a cutting and you needed to remove a few tree roots) and shovels. These last were often so flimsy that they bent if you showed too much enthusiasm. I suppose you can't expect too much from shovels made from fifty-gallon oil drums, and that was where many of them came from because two I saw bore the impression of part of the Shell trademark.

Also required were baskets and/or stretchers made from rice sacks with a hole in each corner at the bottom to take stout bamboo poles for carrying handles.

The path of the railway had been cleared of jungle by a previous party, and surveyors had put up flimsy bamboo guides at intervals to show in section the shape and height of the embankment.

We arrived with our primitive equipment and set to work in parties of six, eight or ten, according to the best arrangement. One in each party loosened the earth with a pickaxe, the next one loaded a stretcher and the next two took the stretcher and dumped its contents in the appropriate place. If digging was easy one pair of diggers could feed three or four stretchers with ease. An onlooker must have been reminded of a nest of ants by our constant hurrying forwards and backwards.

We had a set number of days in which to build a required length of embankment, and the whole affair was worked out on the number of cubic metres of earth required plus the assumption that one cubic metre of earth could be shifted per day per prisoner.

It was schoolboy mathematics: 'How many cubic metres of earth are required to build a section of an embankment 105 metres long, if at A it is to be three metres high, four metres wide at the top and ten metres wide at the base; while at B it is to be four metres high and twelve metres wide at the base?' This would be followed by: 'How many men would be required to do this job in seven days?'

If we finished the job before the given day we had the rest of the time as a holiday. It became the understood thing that a seven-day task was completed in six days, or a ten-day task in nine; even if we had to work halfway through the night to do it. It was the only way we could achieve a Sabbath day in which to rest and to catch up on our washing.

The big snag about such an arrangement is that if you complete the task too quickly, the Japs might add a little bit on when dishing out the next one, and so on until it became next to impossible without killing yourself. We used to see to it that we seldom finished too soon!

On one occasion we had to fill in the embankment to a bridge over a small stream. The Nips must have slipped up badly in their arithmetic for an easy three days' work finished what was scheduled to be a ten-day task. We didn't get seven days holiday, however, for we were sent to help another party where the mistake seemed to have been the other way. We still managed to get an extra day's 'yasmi', so we couldn't really grumble.

At Bankau we found ourselves mixed up with a native village complete with shops and temple. I suppose they looked upon us as the local housing estate dumped down on the doorstep of respectable suburbia.

The shops were really only stalls, and most of these were strung out in a couple of lines, reminding me of Croydon's Surrey Street.

We were being paid twenty-five cents a day now, and what a joy it was to be able to go and spend it at the shops! I rationed myself to spending five cents on bananas (there were three different kinds); five cents on Goolah Malacca (a crude, brown product of the sugar palm, I believe, which tasted sometimes like stiff honey; and sometimes like the stale, dried out pockets of condensed milk lodged in recesses in the top of the tin; and sometimes like 'stickified' Demerara sugar); five cents on 'Chinese wedding cake' (a rather attractive cornfloury, shortbready biscuit) that I really enjoyed; and five cents every three days on limes. That left me five cents in reserve so that I could go rash if I cared to.

These stalls sold a variety of novelties. There were 'banana fritters' – bananas sliced and fried in oil – but they did not appeal to me as you could get twice as much raw banana for the same money. One of our lads suffered a grave misfortune when he experimented on something new and strange. One stall displayed small red pancake-like cakes carefully placed on pieces of green banana leaf. This lad bought one, and was highly disgusted with the taste. Investigation showed he had bought some betel nut paste, which many of the natives chew, to the detriment of their teeth which the paste decays. Betel-nut chewing seems to take the place of tobacco smoking in these parts, and as far as I can make out, the habit is just as enslaving. As far as this English lad was concerned, it was hard-earned money wasted!

I mentioned the temple in our village a little earlier. Of course, it was strictly taboo for us to go too near, although it was in full view if you cared to gaze at it. Like the other buildings round about it was built on stilts to discourage an unwanted congregation of crawling insects. On the platform by the entrance stood a large gong which was struck every sundown. On two or three occasions I stood and watched this performance. It was done by two small boys who thoroughly enjoyed their tasks, the one swiping with boundary-hitting strokes at the gong while the other kept pace with him on some other noise-making instrument. The rhythm seemed to be the important part about the whole affair. They started slowly and sedately and gradually increased in tempo until they were both banging as furiously fast as they could. Bong! Bong! Bong!-bong!-bong!-bong-ong-ong-ong-ong! This was repeated several times and then the rite was over as far as I could see. I have an idea that this is a particularly cunning way of getting rid of evil spirits. You get them dancing to a certain rhythm which you gradually increase until they get going so fast they trip over and go flying off to outer space, or wherever evil spirits go.

The scenery around Bankau reminds me very much of English woodland. At one point our pathway from camp to our particular stretch of embankment passed through a grassy clearing. The first time I passed through it I wanted to take off my coat and put it on the pile of coats that should have been on the ground and join in the game of rounders that should have been going on. What place I was reminded of I cannot remember, but I think it was one of those glorious family reunions where there were plenty of uncles, aunts and cousins, and I was a very small boy. It was reminiscent of a flattened down Croham Hurst, but where there was no view when you came out at the top.

When we finished our work at Bankau, we returned to Wan Ti Kien (One Tuck In) and I was able to check up on the bearings I made on the upward journey. As I said earlier, this was the place where we got plenty of food. This is how it happened.

Like Chungkai, One Tuck In was built by the river. Broadly speaking, our railway followed this river, but like all progressive modernists it impatiently takes short cuts when the ancient waterway meanders round in half-circles.

The Meklong (for so I believe the river to be called after looking at all the small and rather inadequate maps available) is very curly and the railway hops from bend to bend. Where the two meet a camp is found.

The railway lines overtook us while here, and then One Tuck In assumed importance as a transfer point from river to rail of the rations being sent to camps higher up the line. That was when One Tuck In lived up to its name.

Our meat ration consisted mainly of pork, and in order to maintain it, live pigs were sent up. The transport of these animals was about the cruellest thing I've ever seen. Each pig was packed head first in a long tubular basket so that it could do literally nothing except utter vocal protests. Its legs generally slipped through the holes in the coarse basket and because of the rough bundling about it got, were in imminent danger of being broken. It is no wonder that, by the time they reached our camp, the poor pigs were beyond protesting, and often so far gone as to be unlikely to travel further alive. The result was that we killed and ate them while camps further up the line went without. At One Tuck In the chilling death screech of some unfortunate porker was almost a daily affair. The cooks also slaughtered oxen which, although a less blood-curdling affair was nevertheless a brutal business as it had to be done with a sledgehammer and often required a dozen or so blows. At least once the poor beast broke loose, scattering the onlookers in all directions.

I didn't like hearing or seeing any of this, but it meant food for us, and had to be done. As some of the lads pointed out, the death screech of a pig tonight meant a good tuck in for us on the morrow.

When we moved from Wan Ti Kien we had the doubtful luxury of a train journey. A diesel lorry with specially adapted wheels pulled seven or eight light but long trucks piled with stores, and with us perched precariously on top. As we travelled in this comparative comfort, I was impressed with how much an ordinary diesel lorry engine could pull when put on a railway. It was far more efficient than when on the road.

We detrained at Arrowhill (which was as far as the rails went) and hiked the last few kilometres to Bookai. It was one of the worst journeys I've ever attempted. At this point the river ran through a gorge in the hills so difficult that in places there was no room for a respectable footpath – let alone a railway track. A long series of trestle bridges was being put up when we passed, some of them extremely high, and sometimes the only path seemed to be over the sleepers on which the rails were to rest with perhaps a hundred-foot drop if your kit shifted a little and threw you off your balance. This stretch was known as the Wan Po Viaducts, and I should say it was the most difficult piece to build of the whole railway.

The camp for which we were bound was not far from the end of the frightful stretch, but it was quite dark when we reached it. Some of the men behind me were caught in the middle of the viaducts when the daylight failed, and the rest of their journey must have been a veritable nightmare. I'm glad I was not one of them.

We stayed about a month at Bookai building another section of embankment, and cutting a shallow cutting. The soil was of a Devonshire redness, but that did not prevent it harbouring white ants, the nests of which we frequently disturbed. I don't know how they do it but they make their nests as hard as concrete. We dug out a queen ant on one occasion and what a grotesque thing she was! Her head, legs and middle part were normal sized, but her abdomen was extended unbelievably so that she was absolutely helpless. Worse than the ants were the scorpions that gave some chaps some nasty stings. Then there were the nine inch centipedes, as fat as my middle finger, and which were also accused of stinging powers although I never tried to find out. And then there was the tarantula spider with his furry legs.

All the time we were working here, I noticed convoys of butterflies flying in column of route up the track of the railway. They were just like our cabbage whites and came in groups of anything up to a dozen, trying to follow exactly the flight of their leader – a tricky thing for even a butterfly to do. These butterflies used to rest on the ground and several times I came across about a hundred all crowded together on a square foot of soil. When I disturbed them they fluttered up around me like a blizzard of swirling snowflakes!

Life had its funny side, I am glad to say, and we found great amusement in one of our Japanese guards. He was a third-class private, which is just about the lowest form of humanity in the eyes of the Japanese. He was also a very poor specimen physically, and when he took his glasses off, he just couldn't see a thing. The poor little fellow really couldn't sink any lower, but (and this is a very big but) he was the only one who knew any English. Consequently, he found himself exalted to the dizzy heights of interpreter. As such, he was in great demand up and down the long stretch of embankment on which we were working, translating for the various overseers. It was a mixed blessing as he was kept on the trot most of the day. He spoke to some of our chaps and from what they say, I gather he was a student and a really intelligent fellow. He is supposed to have admitted that the Japanese cannot hope to win the war, and to us, that is very heartening.

British soldiers cannot be expected to consider the Nips their friends just at present; but they can be expected to say what they think about them – probably in very unpleasant language. 'Muscle-Bound' (as someone christened this particular little Nip) was dejected when some of our lads swore at him. He sat on a stone and said:

'Japanese officer – he swear at me. Japanese soldier – he swear at me. English prisoner – *he* swear at me. All men swear at me!' Truly his cup of bitterness was full to overflowing. I can't help feeling sorry for that fellow – torn away from his home and his studies to become the butt of everyone's displeasure; and all very much against his will.

Towards the end of our stay at Bookai I went on the sick list with ulcers on my legs. One of them is a bad one, it is an open wound over an inch and a half long and an inch wide. They all seemed to start with small scratches on pieces of dead bamboo and nothing I can do seems to heal them. Treatment for them seems to be little more than bathing them with hot water and resting as much as possible, but although I did this faithfully I was no better when we moved here two days ago. I have a little tin in which I boiled some water in order to soak my rag poultices for drawing the matter out of the ulcers. With my legs rebandaged I retired to my tent and read or catch up on my writing.

Bookai was on a flattish piece of land in a bend of the river. It seems a favourite resort of butterflies and once I found half a dozen different kinds trapped in my tent including one with shiny blue wings such as one sees in butterfly wing pictures. Bookai was also a favourite night haunt of monkeys who regaled us with such a chorus of 'Oooo-ah!' in every different pitch that you might have thought they were playing air-raid sirens. It's not surprising that we nicknamed Bookai 'Monkey Bend', is it?

The journey from Bookai to Tarsoh was a short one but it did not improve my ulcers – neither has the lack of treatment since I arrived.

Tarsoh is a very large camp – a young town in fact – but the area allocated to us was filthy. A consignment of Dutch had passed through just ahead of us and had left the place a veritable flies' paradise. There were no latrines dug and we had to watch our step.

Yesterday I met Eric from whom I had been separated just after arriving in Thailand. A known face in a strange place is better than a ray of sunshine through the thunder clouds, and Eric's proved that to me then, if never before.

He was doing quite well – working in the hospital cookhouse, or some such racket.

'How's Jonny Walker?' I knew he had gone with Eric when we parted.

A sudden change of expression, and 'Haven't you heard? He died last November of dysentery six days after we arrived here.'

Poor Jonny, dead about ten days after I had seen him! There are far too many people dying on this railway.

Well Ernest, that seems to have brought us up to date, and only leaves me with two things more to say. It is obvious that we are only passing through Tarsoh on our way further up the line. Beyond that I know nothing. The other thing is I've not yet heard a thing about you all since I left England so I can only hope you are keeping well.

Love to all at home

Alan

The Railway I Helped to Build

(See illustration on next page)

The direction of the railway after Bankau cannot be considered accurate as it represents adjustments made to bearings taken from the Sun, believed to be wrong. I travelled this section by train in both directions.

From Bankau (the highest camp I reached before entraining for Arrowhill) down to Kanjong-buri the course of the track can be taken as approximately correct. Chungkai was the first working camp I was in and where I was detached from the hospital. From there I went to Wan Ti Kien, stopping one night at Wan Lung. Spent three weeks there (one in hospital) then proceeded to Bankau. While there the rails caught us up, and our task was completed and we returned to Wan Ti Kien for two weeks.

From Wan Ti Kien, train to Arrowhill (then the end of the railway) after which my directions are entirely lost.

I came down as sick from Tarsoh to Bridge Camp (Tamakan) by train, taking twenty hours, which was, I believe, one of the first steam train journeys on this track.

This map, made often by trying to pace distances and taking bearings from the sun, can scarcely claim to accuracy. Note, I even got the name of the river wrong – which is hardly surprising as I only had a very small-scale map to work from.

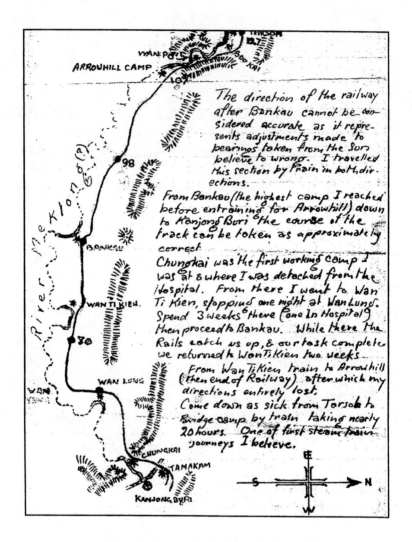

The Railway I Helped to Build
(Copied and Enlarged from Cyclopaedia Nunnica.)

Chapter Seventeen
Fruit for Labour

Tamakan, 10 May 1943

My dear Ernest,

I've just had the privilege of travelling on the railway I helped to build! I can't say I'm proud of my handiwork, but I have a feeling within, which is all the greater as I didn't have to pay my fare.

This is how it came about. I've been sent down country to hospital. I told you in my last letter how I developed ulcers which laid me off work at that outlandish spot called Bookai, and how they were no better when I arrived at Tarsoh. In spite of my protests, I found I had to do another hike – this time on Easter Monday. Fortunately, it was not more than five kilometres.

I really wish you had been with me for once: I am sure you would have seen the funny side of that bank holiday excursion.

We were being sent to join the party putting up the telephone wires, and the economical Nips decided we could take with us a consignment of wire and so kill two birds with one stone. Perhaps I should say bullocks, not birds, for we loaded our precious wire on to thirty one-bullock carts standing waiting in the square. Each cart was inflicted with the kit of two of us as well as the heavy coils of wire. I was promised permission to ride if I could not make the journey on my feet, but the promise was never fulfilled. I hadn't an earthly Ernest! For one thing, there was no room, and for another the Thais would not let me ride at any price. You would be surprised at the inefficiency of those bullock carts. They were built of massive pieces of timber and looked quite worthy of a team of oxen on first sight, but when you notice that you couldn't possibly load on more than three sacks of rice, or six coils of wire, with two men's kit in addition, it makes you wonder why all that beef is required. It strikes me the cattle in this part of the world are 'yaller'. The carts themselves are wonders of creation – never has so much been held together by so little. Nor, come to think of it, has so little been carried by so much. The 'toe-in' of the wheels, just isn't. Instead they 'toe-out' to a most alarming degree. By the end of our journey I came to the conclusion that this is by design and not accident, and that science – condemning such an affair in the swiftly moving motor car – is challenged by the primitive jungle cart expected to move slowly over much be-rutted roads.

In spite of more protests, I had to walk all the way, but it was not very difficult as the pace was nothing more than a dawdle. We started with thirty-one carts, but how many were still with us when we finished our journey I never found out. Before we had reached the foot of the second and final hill we had shed ten by the wayside, needing the wheelwright's urgent attention.

I was fortunate enough to find a cart which at least looked as if it might make the journey in one piece, and put my kit on it. I must be a pretty good ox-fancier, for we reached the top of the first incline with full marks, the oxen showing no ill effects either from exertion or chastisement.

This was no doubt due to the energy I had displayed when a cart ahead got cramp in its off-side wheel and caused a stoppage. Our driver presented me with a fearsome-looking, yet blunt sickle thing with which I reaped a few handfuls of grass for stoking the twin engines. Others were doing likewise (but not as effectively as I, who must collect praise for myself, y'know) so it must have been the normal thing to do, although we had not yet travelled half a kilometre.

There is a funny side to seeing ex-British soldiers industriously cutting wayside grass and applying it to the cattle as though they were feeding camels at the zoo, while the charioteers themselves sit back on their precarious perches and do nothing.

The next hazard was a 'snorter': a steep descent to a narrow be-rutted bridge with a steep, but fortunately short incline to follow. One wagon tried it at a time, four men acting as brakes until the whole affair gathered speed, when, discretion prevailing, they let go and left the contraption to negotiate the bridge the best way it could. Others, with a friendly shoulder and much shouting helped the bullocks up the other side. Again we came up with flying colours. Rather fun this; it reminded one of motorcycle trials back at home.

We reached the foot of the final hill minus ten transports, as I said before. It was long and steep – that is to say, it made a fully laden lorry change down into bottom with respect. For bullocks it was a veritable test hill.

Each cart and pair gallantly charged the gradient. The heads of the cattle nodded slower and slower until even with the aid of the driver's stick and the shouts and shoves of the couple of outriders (as you might call the British lads pushing behind) the useless brutes turned their heads into the hedge, stopped, and began unconcernedly to sample the foliage. Our team must have been the local champions, for with a great display of form we made two-thirds of the ascent with me only pretending to push. To us, the whole show was a right royal competition, and we cheered or jeered according to what we felt to be fit. I was as pleased as Punch when our team climbed the furthest.

After a rest, when the motive force stoked up again with breath and foliage, we carried on to the top. What with the 'smack' of the stick and the shouts of everybody, it must have sounded like Millwall encouraging their centre forward to 'Shoot'.

A pleasant surprise awaited me in the camp at the top of the hill. Hobbling down the stream to a spot opposite the cookhouses where I could wash, I spied Spud Murphy working on the rice boilers. I had not seen him for over a year so I waltzed across to make my presence known. Lo and behold, another surprise! Two others from my unit were working alongside him. They had changed almost beyond recognition.

You can imagine how our tongues started to wag. We hardly had time to answer one question before we were asking more ourselves. 'How's Biggs?' they asked.

'Left him at Changi when I came up; how long have you been here?' I replied.

'October. When did you come?'

'I came up with the hospital in November – yes, Eddie, came up with me – no, I left him at Chungkai with an ulcer on his foot. I hear we have lost some lads up here.'

'Yes, three.'

And so it went on, with me having to repeat my answers to every old face I rediscovered; for I found quite a number of our lads there, and each one was eager to hear all the news.

'Yes, "La-di-da" is up here – he's in charge of the camp. The Nips don't think much of him. They made him parade round with a notice on his back "I am no use to the Japanese".'

In a lowered voice I heard the names of those who so unnecessarily had had their lives sacrificed for the sake of those who grabbed at power and lusted for fame. Such is the price that has to be paid.

'Q' Green was dead – died in the camp above. Although I hadn't forgotten the very unnecessary charge he made against me, I was sorry; for to my mind came the amusing account of how he had brought his family to one of the towns in which we had been stationed at home. Their entrance upon the scene had brought to mind the inevitable army convoy. First had come two children in line ahead. Then mother with the baby, and then at the rear, Pa with the luggage. Q's death was a tragedy to someone.

'Tonchien Sawmills' as the camp was called is prettily perched on the brow of a hill, with an ice-cold stream running through it to fall over the edge as a respectable waterfall. Although we only stayed here four days, and in spite of being sick and staying in camp all day to brew up tea for the boys, it was long enough for me to find a mango tree, see a monkey shot, celebrate the Emperor's birthday and to experience a new, yet old treatment for ulcers.

The mango tree was near where the stream gushed out of a hole in the hillside, just above the camp. Contrary to my expectations I found this particular species to be a colossal tree with the lowest branches thirty feet above the ground. The method of obtaining mangoes was to throw stones up into the branches so that the squirrels, either from surprise or anger, dropped mangoes on to our heads. I saw no squirrels but felt far from safe after a couple of mangoes had dropped with a sizzling 'plomp!' too close for comfort.

The mangoes were not a success for they were hard and under ripe.

The affair of the monkey was much sadder. The monkey (a pure white variety, with long arms and a black face) was up a tree close by unconcernedly getting her lunch. The Nips spotted her, and very soon one of them arrived on the spot gibbering with excitement like a monkey himself as he clutched his rifle. I'll give credit for a good shot. One bullet was sufficient to bring her down without a cry. Like a stone she dropped, long arms making feeble attempts to stop the fall by grabbing at the branches.

In next to no time it seemed, it had been skinned and popped into the cooking pot, while the fur (a neat bullet hole at the base of the spine) was being pegged out to dry. Perhaps you can imagine my feelings after having Jackie as a pet at home.

For the Emperor's birthday we had a 'yasmi', and trivial 'presentoes' were given to the men in the camp. Being strangers passing through, we were just ignored. The Nips drank 'sake' (rice wine) and were very quickly reduced to a state of bawling out their pet patriotic songs at the top of their horribly cracked voices. Experienced topers tell me that when it comes to alcohol, the Nips 'can't take it'.

There's something pathetic about trying to celebrate when you are in the heart of the jungle.

But to return to my ride on the train.

For ulcers, the MI room were using a concoction that I had never heard of before. It sounded harmless and almost stupid – soap and sugar. With all the difficulty of obtaining them it seemed a waste of materials that could have been better employed. Incredulously I slapped on the gauze smeared with the mixture. Next moment I yelped and sucked in my breath as though I had been scalded. I'm glad that my biggest ulcer was only an inch across.

As I said before, we moved after four days. Being sick I was granted the privilege of riding on a truck. I'd rather be fit for the next move even though it means walking. There's a great difference between the main roads at home and the only roads out here. I had to look in the mirror to see if I was grey-haired when I arrived for the bouncing and bumping over roots and potholes made me feel positively aged.

I almost fell off the truck into the arms of the MO who was holding court. He looked at my ulcers, and although I protested I was condemned to be sent down the line back to Chungkai.

Back I went to Tarsoh again by lorry – fortunately a little more sedately. We were parked under canvas close to where I had been the last time I was there; and then followed five days of torture trying to dodge the flies. I took refuge under my two-thirds of a mosquito net after one day; only coming out to collect my meals, or for some other necessary excursion. There was just room for me to lie, and read, or sit and eat my grub.

When it rained, the old tent let the water through, and not content with that, the water swirled in under the brailing, flooding us out. Our kit almost had to swim to keep its head above water. A couple of handy bits of wood and my boots made a precarious perch on which to balance my kit, while a gas cape, crowning the lot, kept the parachute troops from dripping on to it from above. In this way my kit got scarcely more than damp.

I'm not sure whether we welcomed the rain or not, for when it came, the flies were less troublesome.

In the short time I was away from this place, the railway had reached it, and the next part of our journey was to be by train. They had told us that steam engines were operating but it seemed so incredible that I was impatient to see for myself.

When at last we moved, we pressed forward along the path from the camp with more than usual enthusiasm. As I came out of the jungle into the station clearing, the first thing I saw was a real life-size engine hissing away as it pointlessly spilled water on to the track, to the great peril of the embankment. I could see several spots where the embankment had been partly washed away by similar previous behaviour. Obviously, this was meant to be a busy place for there were five sidings. At the moment it was the end of the line as well.

It was one o'clock when we arrived at the station, but we could not start before night fall. I suppose that was because there was so much traffic on the line. At least two trains and a shower of rain arrived while we waited. We crawled under a line of wagons to keep dry – there was no other waiting room.

An engine – our engine it turned out to be – stood close by, fuming as if as anxious to be off as we were. Occasionally it took a turn up and down the siding to ease its aching wheels.

We were packed aboard a line of open wagons long before it got dark, and for an hour or so we expected to move at any minute. It grew dark, and we were yanked out to load up the engine with wood.

We stood in a long chain, passing logs along. I never thought they could pile so much wood on that tender.

When that was filled we started on the furnace. That was an even bigger surprise, for we passed up over fifty logs. We did all this in the pitch dark too. Why couldn't they have made us do it in the light? Then one of our chaps might not have been stung by a scorpion.

At last we started. Out of the siding we puffed with the air of a man who played football yesterday for the first time and is now essaying to pass from bedroom to bathroom without falling to pieces.

Even when the engine had shaken off its stiffness, it still proceeded gingerly. Perhaps it had heard of that other engine that had come off somewhere down the line, and had taken eighteen hours of brute force (and no doubt eighteen hours of swearing on the part of our lads) to replace its wheels on the 'straight and narrow'. Maybe it had heard what one of my travelling companions told me. Misguided and disgruntled Thais had a weakness for removing strategical bits of so-called 'permanent way'.

I was glad we travelled slowly. Many parts of the route were familiar, and the idea of passing certain choice spots conjured up visions of excessive risks to be undergone. There were viaducts and bridges to be crossed; curves to be negotiated; embankments I had built to be traversed. Someone had said the engine had a habit of coming off the rails in awkward places.

The viaducts creaked alarmingly as we crawled over them. One hundred feet below one short bridge I saw an upturned wagon. In places the embankment had been badly washed away by the rains. Also, there were other dangers.

'A guilty conscience conjures up memories, and fear of retribution encourages repentance,' as Solomon nearly said: and to my mind came the picture of a certain little section of embankment in building. It was just where it joined a bridge over a little stream. Somebody scouting around for convenient treetrunks or other suitable junk (to slip surreptitiously into the embankment when the Nips were not looking) found a few boards knocked together to make a concrete mixing platform. When the coast was clear, willing hands had lifted this platform and placed it over a gaping hole in the embankment where it was quickly covered with a thin layer of earth. That had been a real red letter day, for someone else had found a couple of empty beer boxes. Lovely large boxes they were! They had gone in as well, and I remember how the Nip sentry had returned after only the thinnest layer of earth had been sprinkled on top of the last box. To avoid discovery, the officer in charge of us at the time, with great presence of mind, stood on top playing with a shovel as though to pat down some loose earth. There was less than an inch of earth between that box and discovery. We hardly dared to breathe until the Nip passed on.

At the time, this little act of sabotage had seemed a fine thing, especially as we had been able to dodge a little work at the same time: but now that I had to travel *over* that spot, it didn't seem so funny.

Our journey was slow, but to me it was interesting. My native pride swelled up within as I travelled on the railway I had built. Eagerly I sought to recognise the spots where I had shed so much sweat in ant-like toil; curious to know what the engine thought about them. I remembered how, while I toiled, I promised myself a journey on this railway if ever I had the chance, even if I had to go out of my way in years to come: when I was a rich man touring the world.

'Why,' I remembered reasoning, 'should one build a railway if one doesn't travel on it?'

Now, however, I need not travel. I can stay at home (when I eventually get there) and tell how I travelled on the railway I built – with the help of many others. Sweet is the fruit of one's labour, even if it was built by British workmen who were ashamed, rather than proud of their achievement.

That night was clear and starlit. There was comfort in gazing up into the velvety depths (or should I say heights?) of the sky, and picking out the friendly constellations. To the north shone the Plough; and yes the, Pole Star winking away in its solitude like a lighthouse on a barren reef to guide the traveller in unknown and uncharted tracts. Southwards, the Southern Cross was still visible although we are ten degrees north of the equator. Overhead, Orion's belt scintillated bravely, no moon being visible to dim its glory. All clearly told that we were going in the general direction of south-east. That certainly was an interesting point, anyway.

I slept. Cramped up in half the space I wanted, jammed in tight between my neighbour, and with my head doing its best to keep on friendly terms with my haversack pillow, I slept. Not what you would call a good night's rest. I took my boots off and pushed out my legs to fend for themselves, hoping that nothing would land on top of my bad leg.

During one of the rests between sleeping, when I turned my thoughts to the world outside, I saw Christmas trees. Don't laugh Ernest, I saw Christmas trees with their slender foliage and pointed tops etched in black on the dark blue pall of the night, and festooned with fairy lamps. The lamps must have been candles for they twinkled. We passed several of them – God's own Christmas trees! They were an unbelievable sight and hauntingly beautiful, yet wasted on the depths of Thailand's jungle except when a trainload of weary prisoners passes. I'm not mad Ernest – just carried away on the wings of my imagination by a colony of fireflies resting from their nocturnal flight.

The dawn came, and with it a gazing round in search of some familiar landmark. Many times we argued that we had passed Bankau; and many times I recognised the corner around which was the siding from which I had carted rice to Wan Ti Kien.

Argument and memory were both confounded, however, when at last we pulled into what was beyond doubt Wan Lung Station.

'I told you so,' said those who, among many other guesses, suggested that we were not far from this point. 'I knew as soon as I saw that tree with the two trunks growing together into one and forming an arch.' I knew the exact replica of 'that tree' to be near Wan Ti Kien Station.

I suppose it was getting on for nine o'clock when we stopped. The sun had got up but was not yet frizzling us so it could not have been later. Why we stayed there till three in the afternoon will always remain a mystery. It was single track and all that, but there was precious little doing on the up line to stop us.

The sun rose higher in the heavens and we took refuge under the trucks again. By this time we were hungry and no two minds about it. An early tiffin yesterday and a hard-boiled egg to travel with are not likely to keep even sick men from thinking of their next meal. I had had two or three shallots when I started but ate those before we started from Tarsoh with half a cucumber I had picked up from between the rails. With salt it wasn't so bad, but it didn't fill the aching void.

The Nips let us go to fill our water bottles at the well. Past the now-empty barrack huts I went (the camp was deserted apart from the station staff) wondering at the speed with which desolation descends on a place from which man has withdrawn his foot.

I joined the queue waiting their turn at the bucket. To get the water you had to use an ingenious device consisting of two long bamboo poles, one pivoted near one end on which a counterbalance weight was fixed, and the other fixed to it doing duty as a rope by which to lower the bucket. A bamboo 'rope' is a very good idea as you can duck the bucket under the water when you want to fill it. With a rope you have to acquire the knack of dropping the bucket so that the water spills over into it, and that, I find, is very tricky.

The water looked filthy, but it was wet and cold.

Equally important as the well, was the native hut by the tobacco plantation, outside which bunches of leaves were lying in the sun to dry. With an odd ten cent piece I bought some peanuts. They were something to chew even if they did not fill me. Chewing would make me forget how hungry I was. Besides, peanuts are rich in vitamin B.

At last, at long, long last, we moved again, ambling along past scenes which were familiar to me although made strange by the presence of the railway. We passed the quarries at Chungkai, crossing the bridge between them that I had watched a party of officers build – Taramoto's Party they had called it, because they were under the charge of that particularly objectionable person. A minute later we passed the bend where we would have to leave the track to go to Chungkai Camp.

A few hundred yards further on we stopped again. This time there was no siding. Behind us the rails stretched in a straight line towards the hills beyond Chungkai. Ahead they stretched straight forward to goodness knows where. We were surrounded by paddy fields that stretched away on either side as flatly as any part of Lincolnshire, intersected by little foot-high dykes cutting the landscape into little fields scarcely bigger than pocket handkerchiefs. The fields were dry, the greyish mud deeply cracked where the sun had baked it. At our feet we could see the borders of the fields through which the railway had rudely tramped. The holes from which had been dug the earth to build the embankment had collected sufficient water for mosquitoes to breed in. I wondered how much compensation had been paid to the coolies whose fields no longer existed and whose whole living, perhaps, had been lost.

A few sugar palms raised their finely shaped heads on high – too noble to let them sway in the slight breeze they must have found at that height. They lent charm to a scene that, in spite of the sun, would have otherwise looked desolate and uninspiring.

An engine screamed in the distance. At the far end of the line behind us appeared a little black square with a wisp of steam attached. It approached, screaming its annoyance at finding the way blocked. Our engine replied with a wail that clearly indicated he was not to blame for the stoppage, and that he would go on if he could.

Meanwhile we still felt hungry. Eventually we started again. Our journey was nearly done. There was a bridge to cross and then we would be there.

At last we came to the river. I was curious to see what kind of a job they made in crossing it. The engine rallentandoed in respect and gingerly stepped on. I was glad about this, for it creaked in every joint as we passed over.

A little upstream, we could see the new permanent bridge still swathed in scaffolding. From it came the insistent hammer of mechanical rivetters. The bridge appeared to be a thing of huge concrete piers on which rested absurdly fragile looking red girders. They tell me it was brought from Java.

But what was this? We stopped again with our last coach barely back on terra firma; for all the world as if the mental strain of crossing the temporary bridge was too great for our engine's boiler, and it had decided to give up the ghost on the spot.

A Nip guard waved us from the train. We were there! Our journey was completed and 'Thank Heaven!' there was a camp not a stone's throw away. We did not have far to walk on our very empty stomachs.

We were well received, the CO of the camp meeting us personally. He informed us we would have a meal in half an hour. Incredible! There were three hours before supper was due, and surely the cooks wouldn't produce anything before then. They did. Rice with two spoonfuls of sugar (which was twice as much as I've ever had before), together with a mug of tea.

The sun did well to smile down in all his splendour. It really was a grand day after all.

Love to all

Alan

Chapter Eighteen
Prince Bernhart's Birthday

Tamakan, 30 June 1943

My dear Ernest,

I've come to the conclusion that I'm not very patriotic. As most of the Englishmen available at the moment seem to be the same, I don't intend to let this observation worry me. This conclusion was the direct result of witnessing the Dutch doing their best to kick over the traces in honour of Prince Bernhart yesterday.

The first intimation I had of something afoot in the camp was when, in the early morning, I heard the Dutch singing their national anthem – a risky business in a way as the Nips rather object to such displays of patriotic fervour.

The next clue was visible. All the Dutch lads were togged up in their Sunday best, and had just come off parade after hearing somebody spout suitable words and toasting the prince in a tankard of coffee – and, no doubt, trying to get drunk on it if possible.

Of course, such goings on just couldn't be allowed without me wanting to know what it was all in aid of. The answer sent me away reflecting upon the different attitudes of both our nations towards the birthdays of our respective royalty.

Wondering if all were as ignorant as I on the subject. I pounced on the nearest two Englishmen with 'When's the King's Birthday?'

'Don't know.' The first had no pride on the subject.

'Um,' said the second, evidently anxious to impress me that he was not indifferent to the question. 'The twenty-sixth of June or July, I think, but it's not his real birthday – he has that some time in December.'

The next chap I encountered had the confident air of one who had just looked up the answer. 'The third of June,' was his effort. He was unwilling to admit that he had not known yesterday.

Number four said, 'He doesn't know mine, so why should I bother over his?' Unanswerable logic.

I struck oil with a vengeance when I approached a group in one hut.

'Fourth of June,' – said with convincing confidence.

'Third,' corrected his neighbour.

Another plumped for the fourth while the rest remained tactfully silent.

'*Look* here,' said "Third of June", 'I know June like the palm of my hand,' and here he recited a truly formidable list of birthdays, ranging from his own parents, through the extensive field of his uncles and aunts to royalty and others in high places. To this he liberally interpolated a few fixed and moveable feasts, high days, low days, and off days until I found myself surprised that so much could happen in a single month.

After that I decided to give up asking and look it up in *Pear's Cyclopaedia* if I could borrow it.

Meanwhile our well-dressed comrades were trying to work up sufficient enthusiasm to go gay on fresh air. They paraded round in their best dress, refusing to take it off till the day was done. One Dutch sailor stood resplendent in dazzling white. How he did it, I don't know: all my white things still look pale black even after I've washed them; and there's no 'Persil' in the camp.

For once in a while, Dutch singing seemed to prevail in the camp. When it seemed to flag a bit they gave them more speeches in the huts to bolster up enthusiasm for the evening session.

It wasn't much that they did – there was little they could do; but at least they showed their patriotism, which is more than we did. I suppose it's the Englishman's prerogative to appear unpatriotic.

This is, I think, a good opportunity to tell you a little about our Dutch comrades. This is the first camp in which I have rubbed shoulders with them, so I have had no opportunity before of speaking with authority.

In this camp we are roughly fifty per cent Dutch and fifty per cent British. Before I go any further, I had better explain that only a minority of the Dutch here are pure-blooded Europeans. The majority are Javanese, being half-cast, quarter-cast, any cast but outcast, who have decided that Dutch citizenship in captivity is preferable to freedom without it.

Such mixture of the breeds must sound obnoxious to the Englishman who still remembers his old school tie, and the blue blood that flows in his veins; but the Dutch argument on the subject is conclusive. 'They have Dutch blood in their veins and that is good enough.'

When I first learnt of this attitude I thought it a commendable view – right in line with the quality taught by Christianity, etc. But there happens to be a big '*but*'.

In spite of their Dutch blood many of these Asiatics are still decidedly native in their habits. You remember the

Chinese quarter in London – we went through it at least once on our jaunts with a 'Shilling All Day' ticket on the trams during the school holidays – and you know that it is not a model district for cleanliness. It is the home of smells delicious, doubtful and distasteful (chiefly the latter) and can be generally summed up with the term 'squalid'. All that goes to show that even London cannot cure the Asiatic. He is still oblivious to smells, filth, fleas, and discomfort, and will always remain so. Singapore has been aptly described as 'the city of a thousand lights and a million smells'; and that shows you what happens when Europe follows Mohammed's example and goes to the mountains – of Asia.

And so it is with our camp. Mr Javanese, in spite of his Dutch citizenship, is still uneducated in hygiene. Cheerfully he uses his mess tin for washing in; and if at night, he gets 'taken short', he is not above using it to avoid a journey to the latrines. Many of us have used our mess tins for washing, I agree, but we have always avoided doing so where possible, but as for using it at nights 'never'.

Another annoying habit is that of misjudging the distance to the latrine and not making the grade. The thought of covering it over never seems to enter their heads. Unfortunately this is not confined to them, a few Europeans also being guilty of the same. And these things happen, Ernest, in this camp where discipline is rigidly enforced in such matters – and rightly so, for our lives depend on our cleanliness.

Our Dutch friends are very fond of cooking, although we have not been very satisfied with their efforts in the cookhouse. They specialise in private enterprise. They cluster round the little fires they light in the slit trench, specially provided till one is reminded of the flies around the latrine not twenty yards away.

Pass by, and you will be surprised at what they are cooking – and sorely tempted by the delicious aromas they produce on occasions. Peanuts fried in oil are very usual, so are fried and boiled eggs. These are common sights, and if we had the money, we would be doing the same. But when we see tomatoes being fried with onions and I don't know what else (as I saw the other day) I just have to lick my chops and wish I was favoured with such blessings. The smell reminded me of home at breakfast time. Then I got a nose full from twenty yards in the opposite direction.

Every day one can witness cooking and one wonders how they can do it on the working pay we get. One good 'bean-oh' when we spend all our money, yes; but day after day means their being as lousy with money as I am with lice.

We forget that most of our Dutch friends were pressed into the army only a few days before their particular balloon went up to get well and truly punctured. Until the day they were required to use their rifles, they were little more than civilians, and as such had opportunity of gathering a supply of money to carry with them when they became prisoners that made the British soldier appear poverty stricken. None of us had our homes and our businesses handy, from which we could draw sufficient money to keep us going. On the other hand, none of us had houses and businesses to be destroyed by the Japanese.

Those who did some successful looting are rich – some fabulously rich, having their dollars reckoned in thousands when we packed in. Others, who turned their attention to jewellery are now able to realise useful sums of money from the Thais, who see to it that they pay pitifully low prices. In the main, however, we British are poor, and have to sell the shirts off our backs for a little extra cash – that is if we have one that is not in shreds. In contrast to this, the Dutch appear to be well-equipped with money, clothing, and other odds and ends which they turn into these good things that smell so nice.

The Dutchman is 'more fly' than we are, of that I am now convinced. When he is sick, he sees to it that he does not work – not even light work. By hook or (probably) crook he's missing from the fatigue party; and it is left to 'muggins' in the khaki shorts to dig the latrines for the camp, while he with the green shorts (possibly as a result of his culinary efforts) does his level best to fill them up.

In spite of all this, he gives up easily when he is really bad. I believe I am right in saying that most of the funerals are for these Eurasians who seem to inherit the fatalism of the east. I would say that the Dutch funerals out number the British by almost two to one.

And so you see Ernest, we paint our comrades in doubtful colours, and have of many of them a very poor opinion. I cannot think that this is due to those men who have come from that Holland which struck you as so clean when you cycled through it. Indeed, I have becomes very friendly with some of them myself. I feel it must be due to these Eurasians in whom are inbred the habits of the East, and who by their example drag down many to the same level who would be otherwise if not forced to rub shoulders with them.

Love to all

Alan

Footnote:

The terms Javanese, Eurasian, Indonesian, are very muddling to the British Tommy. I have applied these words to half-cast Dutch widely, and maybe incorrectly.

Chapter Nineteen

Constant Companion

Tamakan, 8 July 1943

My dear Ernest,

A man died in our ward during the night. He slept a couple of bays further up on the other side.

Two days ago, just before he went down with a return attack of spinal malaria, he was the envy of the ward, for he received five letters from home.

How my heart thumped when those letters came! Perhaps there will be some more tomorrow. May be there will be one for me. Hope, lying dormant but not dead, sprung up within me like an awakening volcano.

That same afternoon, the attack came on and he passed right out. The orderlies revived him, but he could not eat, could not move, could only shiver under his blanket. He looked bad. We knew he was bad, because the orderlies paid him so much attention. And early this morning, before it was light, he died.

I shall never forget that night as long as I live, for although I was very tired and paid little attention to what was going on around me, certain details are indelibly impressed on my mind.

We had settled down for the night when a choking sort of cough caused someone to call loudly for the orderly to attend the sick man. Gradually, the coughing, together with the murmur of subdued voices that had arisen, subsided; and in a comparative quiet, after breathing a silent prayer for the well-being of the sick man, I feel asleep.

*

I awoke with a sense that it was raining steadily. Habit acquired by many nights under unreliable roofs, turned my first thoughts to the dryness of my bed; but before I could move, another sound was borne in on my senses, the sound of a man groaning spiritlessly with every outgoing breath: 'Erh! Erh! Erh!' Not so much a groan as the kind of grunt one gives when caught unexpectedly by a playful blow in the stomach, only louder and more drawn out. Perhaps it was this, and not the rain that had awakened me. His breathing was rapid. I measured it against mine and found it nearly twice as quick. Certainly he was in a bad way. Was it possible he was about to die?

There was a light by the bed, and I could see a couple of shadowy figures bending over it. A mumble of voices and a figure detached itself from the darkness and went for the doctor.

'Erh! Erh! Erh!' How long would he go on like that? How long could he? Regularly, rapidly, and with no sign of weakening or decreasing the sound went on. 'Surely he can't keep it up all night, perhaps all day as well? By the way, what is the time? Pitch black outside. No moon. No sign of the dawn.'

The noise of heavy feet kicking along the uneven earth floor and four figures pass me with another lamp. The MO. 'What will he do? What can he do?'

The hypnotism of fascination draws my eyes. Someone moves the lamp to look at his face. All I can see is the silhouette of bent heads. Above the subdued voices rises the monotonous, hateful, frightening cry. 'Er-h! Er-h! Er-h! Er-h!' The figures shift and someone is bathing the forehead. 'What's he doing that for?' Of course! Trying to bring down the temperature. I read in a book somewhere that's what they try to do with a fever; ice and all that. But they have no ice, only cold water.

'I'm getting jittery – I'll never get to sleep again if I don't get a grip on myself.' I rolled over and closed my eyes – I really was very drowsy, but I could not close my ears to that voice... 'Almighty God...' I was suddenly wide awake!

A firm, decisive, cultured voice; contrasting vividly with the involuntary cry of the dying man, was praying.

The prayer was short, not more than half a dozen sentences, and the words were mostly drowned. I heard the last part '...Grant that his trust may be in Thee, and that he may enter into Thy peace, for Jesus Christ's sake, Amen.'

The end was near then! He was about to die. The groans grew feebler, and after two or three struggled breaths, which groaned outwards through his lips with, it seemed, a faint note of annoyance, the man lay quiet.

The knot of men about the bed dispersed, leaving only a lamp to continue the vigil. I could not help wondering if the doctor, knowing there was no hope left, had used the needle, helping the already unconscious soul into Eternity with the aid of an injection.

A quarter of an hour passed, and two orderlies returned. I saw one turn back the blanket and feel the heart of the prostrate figure.

'Go and fetch the stretcher.' One of the orderlies repassed my bed. 'Is this all his kit?' A curt question to the patient on the next bed space. The stretcher came and the corpse, lifted by the blanket beneath, and sagging in the middle, was dumped on to it. Back past my bed for the last time they came. Two men carrying a stretcher on which lay a blanket-covered figure. A sight so familiar that the corpse lost its identity and became impersonal. One more body to be laid in the mortuary – one more death.

I could not sleep. More to relieve the strain of taut nerves than of necessity, I crawled off my bamboo couch and made the perilous journey over the rough ground to the latrine.

'What time can it be? The rain has ceased and there seems to be a suggestion of gloaming between the clouds – just sufficient to show how low and threatening the clouds are; just enough to lift the sable blanket of midnight so that I can dimly make out the contours of the ground at my feet, and see somewhat more than the silhouette of the huts around me. It cannot be the moon, for that thin shaving of silver had set before I had settled to slumber last night. Can it be the dawn?'

I turned and looked to the East. A faint but definite glow, a sort of supernatural twilight reflected palely behind the shadowy trees. 'Thank God!' The night was nearly done and the dawn was about to break. Within an hour it would be light; and the world would grunt, stretch itself, and come awake: then I would not be alone with my thoughts.

It was an awe-struck ward when it did awake.

One man, who had been fortunate enough to sleep through it all, spoke to his neighbour. 'He's dead?'

'Died at quarter to six this morning.'

'Who was it?' asked another heavy sleeper.

'That chap down there in the second bay; you know, the chap that received all those letters the other day.'

Instinctively they look towards the empty space.

'What was his name?' I asked.

'Don't know. He comes from Lowestoft – I was talking to him about there only two days ago. And to think he received all those letters too – I wonder if there was any bad news in them.'

The letters, however, had contained good news – let us hope that they comforted his dying thoughts.

'Poor —,' said another, not in a jest, nor in anger, but because his tongue by habit found foul words, and this was his way of expressing his earnest sympathy. 'He just let hisself go.'

They buried four after breakfast. The drama of the night that I had witnessed, had been repeated in all its grimness in three other places unknown to me. A drama which went on around me every day – known to me, and yet to which I was a stranger. It was not surprise that a man had died that held us spellbound – one might almost say we expected it. What did seem wrong was that someone should die in our ward – the scabies ward – where nearly everybody was moderately fit and no one ever looked like dying. One could almost gamble on someone dying in ward nine on the isolation side of the fence, as on a certainty; after all, dysentery has accounted for half the deaths in this camp. Whenever a man is carried to that ward we subconsciously take his death warrant as signed.

Callous? I suppose it would seem so to you. War makes you like that and for the last month we have been conscious of such a tenseness as is only felt by men in action – men who know they are fighting for their lives. Our enemy is not the Imperial Japanese Army this time, but disease. Here is an enemy far more potent, far less visible, that strikes in the dark with unseen hand over a front of undefined length and depth. The working camps a hundred miles up the railway are in the front line. There the battle rages fiercest and men are dying in scores. There, a man speaks to his friend in the morning and by tiffin time they are burning his body as loathsome refuse. There, men are being worked to exhaustion and starved to weakness, till their resistance is broken down and they fall easy victims to disease.

Thus it has been since the day we surrendered, but never have the odds been so heavy against us.

Dysentery and malaria first took the field while we were at Changi. In support came malnutrition. Diphtheria came next with a lightning thrust attended with great success. Beri-beri consolidated the position. Then came the final blow, more powerful, more overwhelming than any that had come before – cholera – the dread of these tropical lands, sweeping away hundreds before a finger can be lifted to prevent its course. And ever in support, working behind the lines, and undermining our defences – malnutrition.

Our camp is like a rest camp and hospital behind the front but close enough to be in danger from the enemy's long range weapons. Here we receive the men who have broken under the strain and are unable to carry on working. Here we fight with medicine and disinfectant, food and strict regulations, the diseases in our midst. Here we stave off the cholera that is threatening us.

Oh, how pitifully insufficient are our medical supplies, and yet they exceed the wildest dreams of the doctors in the working camps. The medical officers in this camp, and even more especially in working camps up the line, deserve the highest praise for the courageous way they have fought on, their hands tied by hopelessly inadequate supplies; their skill tried by the appalling conditions under which they work. Their work should receive public recognition.

I'm no medical man Ernest, as you know, and cannot write authoritatively on this medical war – I must leave that to the doctors themselves – but what I do know is that it deserves a place of prominence and honour in the annals of medical history. I do know the doctors are fighting against overwhelming odds. They fight on, knowing they can do so little; gripped by a despair that makes them cry out at times, 'I could save that man if I had the right medicines.' That big little word 'if'. We in the rank and file may never know how much pride the doctors and senior camp officers are pocketing in order to wheedle supplies of vital drugs out of the Japs. How some of them hate themselves while they kowtow to these little yellow men in order to curry favour – favour that might win some drugs for us. And the Japanese make a poor ally in this war, against disease. The other day a hundred men arrived from up-country. I wish you could have stood with me near the gate as they came in, the Japanese guard spraying with disinfectant as they file past. They gather in ragged lines near us, waiting to be told where to go. Here comes a man, as thin as a lath, and hobbling on a stick, his legs swathed in dirty bandages. He is ragged and dirty, and carrying all he possesses in a small haversack slung over his shoulder.

Behind him come two apparently robust men, supporting between them a man who looks, and is, exhausted. Now a man with a bandage over one eye; now one with his right arm off at the elbow. Four orderlies bring in a stretcher carrying a ginger-haired lad.

And so they come, worn out not so much by the journey as by disease. Look at their faces before they move off to their huts. Dirty and unshaven, they look at us with the same curiosity we bestow on them. Many show joy and curiosity at seeing fresh faces and hearing news of friends, and some even crack jokes; but for every face so seen, there is another in which the eyes are the dominant feature – a drawn face in which the eyes seem to be peering anxiously into the distance – haunting eyes staring from spiritless faces.

From them we can gather some idea of what they have been through, and we humbly thank God that we came down country before conditions had becomes quite so bad.

I remember seeing faces like these once before – in France it was, and they belonged to the broken and battered remnants of Belgium's army after they had been overwhelmed by the Jerries. So spiritless that their owners greeted my optimistic 'thumbs up' with a disheartened 'thumbs down' as our trains passed.

We wonder how many of these men will die and how many will recover. One cannot help but grow callous when rubbing shoulders with death every day.

Scarcely a day passes without the funeral cortege being seen with the Dutch padre stepping out in front in his familiar green uniform, followed by the fatal, red ensign-covered stretcher on which can be seen the contours of the corpse – the rounded head with a valley at the neck followed by a more gradual bulge, tapering away to the feet which thrust up the pall to a little red pinnacle. Every funeral uses that red ensign because its the only flag in the camp. You know it's not a British funeral because the bearers are in green – they would be in khaki if it was British.

No one is surprised; no one is deeply shocked now. Everyone accepts the scene as normal and inevitable. So would you if you could come with me and peep into ward seven and see some of the men for whose lives we are fighting. Surely it is impossible for them to be any thinner!

They are skin and bone already, and they are still wasting away with dysentery.

One, here on a stretcher, looks bad – so bad he hasn't even the energy to brush away the flies that settle on his bare arms. He stares at us with lustreless eyes that persuade us that it is too great an effort to think. Our unspoken thought is 'How long before he dies?', and although our hearts may be torn with compassion over his disease-ravaged body, the thought of his death leaves us curiously unmoved.

Walk down the gangway and see how many faces wear that fatal stare, vacant and terrible, and speaking of hope lost and the struggle abandoned. A stare suggesting death even while life remains.

Can you imagine the thoughts of a patient in that ward? Bereft of every comfort and crammed like sardines on the uneven bamboo beds so closely that your neighbour kicks you when he rolls. Little but water to eat because you are on fluids. A cut down petrol tin with its edges still jagged doing duty for a bedpan. A sickening stench that makes one hold the breath and overpowers the smell of disinfectant. Above all, a neighbour who has only hours to live, and whose breath comes in noisy gasps. They do not always die as easily or quietly as the man in our ward either. Many times I've heard the delirious shouts and maddened cries of a man whose course is nearly run. Death is a constant companion here; stalking where he will with no one strong enough to say him 'nay'; and we feel he has been wondrously cheated of his prey by every patient who leaves the ward alive. It must be an earthly hell!

Thank God I've not had dysentery!

Twelve hours ago a man lived – now, he's been buried nearly eight. Time is so relentless. Life is so fragile. Death is so awful. I feel as in a dream!

I carried water into hut number nine the other day.

With a smile, I asked one man what book he was reading; trying to appear interested in him. Fixing his vacant eyes on me, he tonelessly told me, adding a query as to whether I wanted to buy it.

I told him I was not interested in it, but he pressed me, 'Buy it, then you can always sell it again, perhaps at a profit.'

I was firm, so he changed the subject: 'Had I any cigarettes?' 'No.'

His reply represented me as unreasonable, and he turned impatiently from me. He was very thin, and I couldn't help wondering if he had given up hope. He seemed like a man literally dying for a smoke.

Perhaps, as I write this he has already died. Maybe I have seen his flag-covered body pass out the gate as I stood to attention in respect of another whose life has been wrested from him in the service of his country.

Love to all

Alan

Chapter Twenty

The Activity of the Idle

Tamakan, Monday 6 September 1943

My dear Ernest,

I'm hobbling round like an old man of ninety. Not that I've suddenly aged – only that I've sprained my ankle rather badly while playing volleyball on Saturday; and now I have to use a couple of sticks to get around. This means I shall be pretty 'static' for a few days, which will give me time to tell you a little about the life here, and how I came to be playing volleyball.

The Nip commandant is a very decent chap I'm thankful to say, and has allowed us to do many things to amuse ourselves.

Although ours is a hospital camp, there are a lot of fellows here who have got fit again, and who do various jobs for the Nips outside the camp. Police, cooks, watercarriers, etc. On yasmi days there is plenty of sport for those who care for, and can take part in it.

Within our limited bounds we have found room for a well-shrunken football pitch, courts for volleyball, basketball, badminton, and a – you'll never believe it, as I thought my eyes were playing tricks when I saw it myself – nine-hole golf course, miniature of course! Admittedly, golf clubs are home-made, and marvellously unconventional, and resemble miniature croquet mallets used sideways instead of end on.

It's football that is the biggest attraction, however, and believe me when I say we've had some exciting games to watch. English-Dutch Internationals almost produce nervous breakdowns, especially when the scoring is very scarce. On a pitch this size (scarcely more than half the length of a full-sized pitch) you can hardly talk of mid-field play; for if we are not pressing their goal, our own castle is in imminent danger of falling. When the Dutch goalkeeper took a goal kick, our goalkeeper had to keep his eyes skinned. The ball usually landed about three-quarters of the way down the pitch – possibly close to a Dutch forward. I've even seen our goalkeeper have to save it from going in his own goal! That Dutch goalkeeper was sensational! He was one of these lads with a generous mixture of Javanese blood in his veins, and although he played barefooted, he could outkick everyone else in the camp.

'Throw-ins' were another source of danger. Some chaps could easily throw into the goal mouth from the touch line, and a throw-in down near your opponent's goal was infinitely more dangerous than a corner.

The most outstanding game I have seen was an English-Scotch International, in which – to use their words – they 'showed us how to play football', beating us by a narrow margin. You should have heard the arguments the match produced in the various wards afterwards. The Scotch supporters said something about the way Scotland always put it across England at football – and has done so for I don't know how many years. England's reply was a reminder of the occasion within the last ten years when England won four-nil (or was it 4-1?); which no Scotsman seems to have remembered. Lack of adequate proof kept the argument going for days.

That's what happens to most of the arguments here. If *Pear's Cyclopaedia* doesn't cover the answer (and I may say that it does very well and rises to the occasion with commendable frequency) then we have to fall back on the principle of 'my word against yours', which can be enlarged to 'my friends' and 'my word against yours and your friends' word' *ad infinitum*.

Another outstanding feature of this place is the pavilion. There is a remarkably good attempt at making a raised stage complete with proscenium arch and wings in front of which we can gather and watch the shows and other diversions that are put on for our amusement or distraction.

Very little initiative has been shown by the officers in providing such amusement or distraction for those who are ill. True, one is in charge of the concert party, which goes round the wards giving shows as well as more magnificent performances on the square, but according to the lads themselves he's more trouble than he's worth.

Apart from this and sport one or two of us have got things going in our spare time. The padre is doing Herculean work, sparing some time for us although he really has his hands full with his Dutch flock. Two lads, Cassidy and Page, conduct services in the wards on Sundays, and I am very pleased to be able to help them with these. During the week, both of them have got their sidelines.

Jock Cassidy has organised a 'Stedfast Club' for old members of the Boy's Brigade, and he has roped me in as an hon. member and vice-president; so I'm a person of importance now. Jock has gathered quite a following. He has issued us with attractive membership cards with the badge of the club on the front and necessary details inside, terminating with the padre's signature.

Ginger Page on the other hand has launched the camp choir to aid in the ward services. Here again I've 'clicked' for high rank in the shape of assistant conductor. Ginger knows a lot about enthusiasm even if he knows very little about reading music. I don't claim to be so very good myself, but I stand by and teach the tenors and basses their parts. Even so all the credit must go to Ginger for making a presentable singing band out of the rawest of material – my goodness, was it raw! The choir's chief use is to focus attention on the services we hold to supplement the padre's efforts. Being nothing more than a corporal and a couple of lance-jacks we feel we need a little publicity.

Mind you, I'm sure we could have got all the publicity we wanted if we advertised the fact that between us we represented three different denominations, which, when said quickly together in one breath sound particularly paradoxical – Plymouth Brethren, Methodist and Mormon. However, we claim to be 'interdenominational' and base our union on the Gospel of Jesus Christ as shown forth in the Bible. We maintain no sectarian barriers in public, and strange as it may seem, things work out smoothly, and we know our efforts are appreciated.

Two Sundays ago we had the pavilion for a community hymn singing service. This was conceived in the first place as our answer to the threat of Sunday concerts, towards which there is a growing tendency. We excelled ourselves, with 'Lead Kindly Light' as the highlight, supported by solos of 'Comfort Ye My People' (*The Messiah*) and 'The Lost Chord'.

We were billed to put over another such service last night only rain stopped play. Yours truly was to be soloist, singing *Jerusalem*. We went into 'I' ward instead and went through our repertoire to an appreciative audience. My solo was left out, and Jock was roped in to give a short address. I'm afraid I can hardly call the listeners a congregation as they seemed to resent rather than approve of Jock.

I've told you what Ginger and Jock have as sidelines. I've mine as well. When I feel equal to it, I go into the worst wards – the dysentery cases – and try to cheer them up with a word of comfort and cheer. You should see the way a face lights up – a face attached to a body which you know could not move off its bed – when I ask whether the owner will be able to walk to the boat in a week's time. 'I'll have a good try!' comes the reply.

In one ward I've started reading a book, and they look forward to it. There should be more of this reading aloud, I think: it seems to be just what's wanted. We really need somebody to make it their job to organise such things, and not leave it to chaps like me to do it off our own bats. So that I can get through the fence that divides our camp in two I have made myself a Red Cross arm band with 'Asst. Chaplain' on it. I feel this to be quite in order, although I've had no official sanction, as I take my New Testament with me so that I can converse on spiritual matters.

Lectures are often organised in the wards, but here again they lack system and appear most haphazard. Even the Bridge and Chess tournaments failed at the end, in my opinion. One can hardly blame the Australian sergeant who organised them, for doubtless he found it a heartbreaking job. It's very difficult to do things like this without an officer's rank to back you up.

Since the Chess tournament (in which I discovered I was one of the strongest players in the camp) I've been playing quite a bit of chess when I feel like it. It's one of the best ways of passing the time when you've nothing to do and all day to do it in.

I've not neglected my reading either. I've just read *Les Misérables* by Victor Hugo and found it a marvellous book, although the means of making me feel thoroughly squashed. While in my possession I lent it to a Dutchman who read far quicker than I could and who returned it with the comment 'Not so good as in the original *French*!' Was I squashed!

I own two very good books at the moment – Daphne du Maurier's *Rebecca* and Neil Bell's *The Desperate Pursuit* – and with these I can command the best books in the camp. One or two good books by noted authors have come my way, including *The Stars Look Down* and a political book by Duff Cooper. I'm hoping to get *Gone with the Wind* soon.

There is no doubt about it, a lot can be learnt from good books, and I'm glad to say there are plenty in the camp. It's a mistake to ignore this aspect of one's education as I have tended to do. If one wants to hold one's own with people a literary background is a great help. Without it, one does not seem properly equipped and is as bad as a soldier going into action without his 'first field dressing'. It might not be required, but its presence gives confidence to face emergencies with some degree of calmness.

But why am I lecturing you? You are the schoolmaster, not me. Talking like this must mean I've nothing else to tell you. As a fact I haven't at the moment. All that's left is for me to say that we are still keeping up our 'peckers', and that the news (rumours) we get is good.

Love to all

Alan

Membership Card of the Stedfast Club

MEMBERSHIP CARD	THE BOY'S BRIGADE
NAME... NUNN	:OBJECT:
UNIT... 251/85 A/T Rgt RA.	The advancement of CHRIST'S Kingdom among boys, and the promotion of habits of obedience, reverence, discipline, self-respect and all that tends towards True Christian Manliness
RANK... L/bdr.	
B B Coy...	
B. B. RANK... +	
CHURCH... Ross Rd Hall Brethern	
HOME ADDRESS... 93 Warrington Rd. Croydon, Surrey. (Eng.)	
Caulsland PADRE	Founded 1883 BY Sir William A Smith
(signed) LEADER	

N° 957891
HON. MEMBER
31

Stedfast Club Member's Details

Chapter Twenty-One

The Monsoon Breaks

2 October 1943

My dear Ernest,

At last, at long long last it's broken. I think no one will deny it this time. Mind you it's been threatening for some time, but now it's broken beyond repair. When we were at school we learnt all about the monsoons and how they arrive as regularly as clockwork. One felt, to hear the teacher carry on so, that one could set the calendar by it. Perhaps you are teaching your unfortunate pupils the selfsame thing.

As I have told you already, I did not get very far into Malaya when the fighting was on. Fellows that were up in the north came back with tales of the rain pouring in rushing torrents or relentless trickles for days on end.

Singapore was different, although it was supposed to be in the thick of it. In fact they claim they get a double dose; catching the north-east winds in the chest and the southwest on the rebound when the wind belts shift around.

From what I saw, Singapore gets a broken monsoon every other month. When I arrived in Thailand, the first thing I heard was that the monsoon was over. At any rate, the rains were not in session. We could expect two or three reasonably dry months.

If we were inconvenienced by mud or damp beds we counted our present blessings and said: 'Just wait till March – when the rains come!'

March came – and went. And with it came the information that next month we would see enough rain to make us sick.

May found us telling one another that the monsoon was late in breaking this year.

And so the months rolled by, till now, when, punctually on the stroke of midnight on the first, those who predicted October as zero hour (or month) were gratified to hear the rain teeming down. It has rained for thirty-six hours since then, with now as the first glimpse of a hazy sun through a thin patch in the overhanging curtain of white and grey clouds.

Frankly Ernest, this tropical weather has me mystified. Here I expect to do what everybody tells me one can do in the tropics (foretell the weather for weeks ahead), and yet I might just as well be in England for all the settled weather we are getting. You stand just as much chance of getting a day's cricket spoilt here as you do in Manchester.

I've been looking up statistics for rainfall in an atlas and I find that September is supposed to be the wettest month in Bangkok, with October second with only half as much. By the end of this month we should be set at 'fair' for the next two months. I suppose we will have rain then. I've been agreeably disappointed over the rainfall in this part of the world. I expected more. The drier the weather the less mud there is to plough through, and the less chance there is for the rain to come sneaking through the roof to wet what little kit you have. The life we are living at present is essentially out in the open air. If you want to see a concert or hear a sermon, even if you want to get your grub – to say nothing of seeing the proverbial man about his proverbial dog – you must leave your precarious shelter and go out into the blinding sun or driving rain according to whichever happens to be in operation at the time. At home, I suppose, you are rather apt to lose sight of such small facts as there being no opening for a firm of window cleaners out here, which gives me the opportunity to pun horribly by saying that openings are just what our windows happen to be. I've not seen a pane of glass since I became a prisoner of war. In our huts, the wind (and the rain if it gets half a chance) comes whistling in, and there's nothing you can do about it.

Just now I mentioned concerts and sermons, which as a rule don't mix very well in one breath. In this camp we've mixed them a lot in our conversation, and its all because of the 'pavilion' which I mentioned in my last letter.

Calling it the pavilion gets round the difficulty of deciding whether it's a church or a theatre. It gets called either quite indiscriminately. Built in Dutch style with a double-pitched roof and retiring rooms on either side of the raised floor that makes an excellent stage, it seems especially designed for producing concerts. Perched up high in a conspicuous position in front hangs a cross made from bamboo, which clearly gives the ecclesiastical touch. There we have the material which kept discussions going (often rather heated I'm afraid) night after night with no padre handy to step in and settle the matter out of hand by repeating the rather dirty trick worked at Singapore.

This particular incident was told me during the discussion of Tamakan's problem. Apparently, some of the lads built up what was intended to be a theatre, with seats and all. Along came the padre and held a service in which he consecrated the place, lock, stock, and barrel. Being consecrated put an end to all ideas of using it for concerts. Imagine the rage of the baffled architects!

Here at Tamakan we only have the Dutch padre, and he would not commit such an undiplomatic act; so the matter was not dropped. Some of the concert party objected to performing under the shadow of the cross, considering it sacrilegious. In the end the cross was taken down for concerts and put back again afterwards. Then, as no one raised any objections (especially the Nips who are supposed to have given permission to build a church but not a theatre), they just didn't bother to put the cross back one day, and there it lies in HQ office at this very moment.

What has all this to do with the monsoon? Simply this. Whereas the star turn, be he preacher or player, is nicely sheltered, his hearers are left out in the open to receive showers of blessing in another form. Such showers as they are most anxious to avoid.

We had a Scottish night there the other night – run by Jock Cassidy and the BBs. The stage was beautifully decorated with tartans scrounged from the kilts of the Gordons and, and an officer's blanket which looked like an amateur imitation of the Buchanan tartan. Everything except the weather was set at fair. Show and shower started simultaneously (nice little tongue twister) and the crowd disappeared. The show went on, which I thought was a really stupid thing to do. It should have been kept for a fine day.

The rain put off our choir 'do' twice, but the third Sunday turned up trumps and was attended with fair success.

You will appreciate, Ernest, that we have been looking forward to this monsoon with great misgivings. It now seems to have set in, so I suppose we shall have pure misery for two or three weeks, at the end of which we shall all be suffering from pneumonia, rheumatism, and other hard to spell complaints, to say nothing of real army troubles like trench foot and drenched clothes.

Tonight I am going to run another 'Guggenheim' in the ward, which will probably mean I shall get splashed with rain dripping through the roof. The rain has eased off a little at present – but I wish this blue-pencilled monsoon would stop!

Love to all
Alan

PS

4 October. Have not been able to post this till now so have just time to say that the monsoon must be over as it did not rain yesterday and today has also been fine. Things definitely look brighter in more ways than one.

Chapter Twenty-Two

Letters from Home

The Beech, Conquitor, Near Burma Frontier
23 October 1943

My dear Ernest,

'Nunn!' I looked up from under my mosquito net (which I had rigged up to keep off the flies) with the slightly annoyed expression of a chap who is just expecting his officer to detail him for some fatigue. The officer smiled: 'Three letters for you.'

And that's how I received my first news from home since I stepped on the train two years ago that whisked me away to Glasgow en route for this dump here.

I was surprised. Ever since I nearly died of heart failure a few weeks ago at Tamakan, I've told myself that none of my mail will ever reach me until I am free.

'Died of heart failure?' you ask. So would you nearly, if you had been sitting on your bed writing when a voice softly queried 'Bombardier Nunn?' I looked round to see a runner from the office holding some letters in his hand. My heart did its best to stand on its head and force its feet out of my mouth.

'Can you tell me,' pursued the wayward youth when I informed him his deductions were correct, 'where Brown

F. W. out of the Cambs, and Harris J. E. from the Norfolks sleep?' (These names are fictitious.)

If I hadn't been too busy dying of sorrow on top of shock, I'd have got up and slaughtered him. Perhaps I should explain that he came to me as I was ward clerk, and handled the list of names of people in my ward.

This time however, it was 'the real McCoy' (to use an unaccountable army expression): I had three letters actually in my hand. I hardly knew whether to finish my dinner or to sling it into the river. I decided to read as I ate.

There was one from mother and two from my beloved wife. The latest date was October 7th, which meant that they were over a year old. Still, that meant that after nearly a year away from home, you were all well; which means a lot to a chap in my position. I looked for items of news.

'I received your air mail letter from Singapore.' That's news to me. I forgot I had ever sent it. I wrote two or three times from the island, but which one did I send by air mail? All that matters is it was received. Good!

Hullo! here a bit heavily censored in black, and a good job made of it too. 'Gordon is —' Hum! Somewhere he shouldn't be, I suppose. Anyway who *is* Gordon? It's two years since I sorted out all my wife's friends and relations, and I've had ample time to forget them. Gordon? Cousin I believe; in the Home Guard – or was it the RAF? Give it up and pass on.

'I told you all the news in my other letters.' Very helpful indeed, as the others seem to have gone astray. I don't ever expect to get them now. I've heard rumours of some thousands being destroyed by water, and other thousands being burnt. Other rumours suggest large quantities of letters stored in various camps where for some reason or other they are not being sorted yet. 'Maurice has just had the rest of the wedding photos done!' What photos? I thought I had seen them all. 'Cutting the cake has come out well.' I don't remember that one at least. Just done? Why have they taken nearly a year to develop?

'I have been wondering about you being able to get clothes and things, and am very relieved to hear the Red Cross have got parcels to Singapore.' So writes Eileen. She wouldn't worry if she saw me running round in a 'Jap-happy', just like any African native. The biggest worry I have about clothes is how to carry them about when I have to hike. The next worry is how to prevent my 'mates' pinching them. As for Red Cross parcels, very few have received them. I don't suppose it matters much, however, as a nice woolly muffler, with woollen gloves and balaclava to match would be very little use out here, except to unravel and sell to the Nips so that they can knit stomach protectors. In this way we console ourselves over their absence.

There is one real item of news. It suggests that you might soon be putting your fetlock into wedlock with 'Rene' (I hope I'm not saying something I shouldn't). If you go and do a thing like that I'll be properly up a gum tree with a sister-in-law I don't know, but dimly fancy I may have seen. Is she the sweet young lady to whom I was introduced on the houseboat?

A year has elapsed since the letters were written; and with a shock comes the realisation that even now you may be married. You may even – I may even be an uncle!!!

So you see Ernest, my letters contained very few details of real news. But what do details matter when I learn the all-important fact that you are safe and well! Many are the questions I would like answered, but I have no cause for complaint. What need I more than the confidence Eileen expresses in one of her letters – 'England is still England and always will be, never fear darling!' Or the comfort of 'We hardly know there's a war on.' Or again, the delightful words of love reassuring me that I am not forgotten, and that my return is longed for!

My new address has no doubt mystified you. Just the same as it mystified me when I set out to come here. I got caught for a draft going up-country. I thought all the work had been done; but no, a few more kilos required doing.

It took four days by train (two by steam and two by diesel), and another day's hike before we joined our party at the 248 kilometre mark. The party was putting up telephone wires, and we almost arrived too late. When we started work, we completed the task in four days. It seemed very queer after struggling through the jungle and hooking wire over telegraph poles, to come upon a pole from which the wires stretched tautly away as if in the heart of civilisation. Silent witness that somebody had been there before.

We changed camp once, carrying our kit about eight kilometres to our present camp in a bend in the river. Not very far away are some mountains – they must be mountains for there is no vegetation clinging to the top. They look very strange after the hills further down the line, every inch of which is claimed by the jungle that rears its vegetation, proudly above the crests of even the sheerest slopes; giving the whole a very shaggy look. I believe these mountains are in Burma, and that gives me that hypnotic feeling I never fail to experience when I gaze across land or sea at another country.

We've finished our work now, and are sort of marking time until they find out what to do with us. We do not grumble, for a lot of 'yasmi', interspersed with a little maintenance and a bit of fishing, suits us. The Nips make bombs with a stick of explosive in a piece of bamboo and a length of fuse, which they light and throw into the river. The blast kills or stuns the fish, and then we dive in and pick them out. We may get about a hundred good-sized fish, which we share. Very entertaining and profitable. Last time I got a small one for myself which I tried to sell to the Tamils for a dollar. They wouldn't have it at that price so I grilled it myself. Some who collared more fish made as much as four or five dollars out of their catch. The cookhouse share went into the stew which was rather a bad thing as it was difficult to mind the bones.

Well Ernest, we expect to move soon – any day in fact, so you must look out for my next letter from a different address. In the meantime I think I had better read through my letters again.

Love to all

Alan

Section Traced from Rangoon to Bangkok Railway

(See illustration on next page)

Specially printed for released prisoners of war and internees.
Printed by 63 REP GROUP September 1945.
Scale 1:1,000,000
1 inch = 15.78 miles
This presumably shows the official names and spelling of the camps on the railway.

All names from Rukke to Three Pagodas Pass have been stuck on an already prepared map with the exception of ThaSao and Dha Khamun. Near Bankau and Wampo names appear to have been removed. Chungkai does not appear, but Whang Khahai, written across the area in bold type with no locating spot, is probably it.

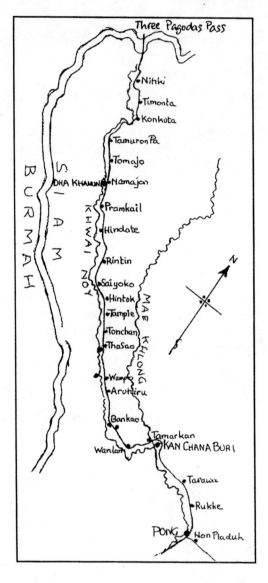

Section Traced from Rangoon to Bangkok Railway

Chapter Twenty-Three
The Housing Problem

Takanun, Saturday 4 December 1943

My dear Ernest,

Seeing I've had an easy day today I have time to scribble you a few lines. I've been doing my level best to do a little work and make it look like a lot. The camp QM, bless him, gave me a broom to play with, some vague instructions and a wink, and left me practically to myself. I applied the first rule one learns in the army, and 'made myself scarce'. Result – a nice, lazy day.

This was quite a change from yesterday when I was out 'on wood'. The work here is planned so that we spend one day in camp doing all sorts of jobs, and the next day we go out chopping wood for the railway engines. The idea is an easy day and then a hard day. One day in camp and the next day out. The only trouble is that you are likely to work harder on the easy days than the hard. Wood cutting is considered hard. When on wood you have a task to do. A party of ten is expected to produce a pile of half-a-metre logs four and a half metres long and a metre high. When you finish that (often just after tiffin), you go back to camp and finish for the day. On camp fatigues you work till six o'clock (and often later), which is not my idea of rest, especially when the work is just as hard, as it sometimes was.

About a week ago we moved into our new home – a brand new attap and bamboo hut that we have just built, and which has the distinction of being the highest and most jerry-built hut in the place. We had been put in leaky old tents when we arrived on November 18th (when I received another letter from Eileen) and had been set on building this hut. It's certainly not an advertisement for British workmanship, as anyone would agree if they had been here when the wind blew the other day. The hut swayed and creaked so much that we had to hold the roof down and the hut up.

I can assure you some of the building material is not really strong enough because I spent a week going up the local hills cutting bamboo poles. We were sent out in small parties with instructions to bring back three large bamboos each, and the sooner we could do this, the sooner we finished our day's work. You will hardly blame us going for the easiest to cut, irrespective of whether they were strong enough.

I am relieved and glad to tell you, however, that to date the hut is still standing. I hope it keeps up till after Christmas as I don't want to spend Christmas day building huts. We are to have a 'yasmi' then, and we're already preparing for 'big eats' by setting aside some of our working pay for the purchase of extras.

I've joined the choir here, and am in the process of learning carols. It's a good choir and we have been tackling some really difficult pieces. It is composed mostly of officers, and is conducted by a man who has something to do with Ely Cathedral Choir, I believe. In short, I've enjoyed one or two good sings.

Later, Wednesday 16 December 1943

Today we have an unexpected, and to me, very welcome surprise, as it gives me an opportunity of finishing this letter.

This morning was occupied with the most amazing religious service it has ever been my privilege to attend. It was a joint commemoration service in which not only the English and Dutch participated but also the Nips! It was held in the cemetery under the shadow of the large wooden cross, erected 'In Memory Of Our Fallen Comrades'.

I wonder if you can visualise that scene, Ernest. The inevitable hollow square of the drum-head service, with the memorial cross in the place of an altar. To the left rear stood the choir. From there I could see squads of Nips on either flank, and beyond them the dilapidated khaki of British troops. The far wall was composed half of khaki and half of the green of Dutch uniforms. Chairs had been placed for the Japanese officers in front of their own men, and a table from the office did duty as a rostrum.

I'll not weary you with a detailed description of this service. There were the usual hymns and prayers and laying on of wreaths that one expects at such services of remembrance, as well as a magnificent speech in jerky Japanese by the colonel in charge of our group of POW camps. This was delivered from the top of the specially placed office table. The interpreter told us that Colonel Yanageeda lamented the loss of 1,130 men in our group of camps during the building of the railway. After this, he and his fellow officers laid wreaths at the foot of the memorial cross. The number of casualties seems surprisingly small.

I'm still wondering how many months ago that list was published.

Don't get me wrong about Colonel Yanageeda, Ernest. I believe he was sincere in his expression of sorrow. Ask anybody who was in group II camp, Thailand, if ever you meet them, what they think of the 'little colonel' and I'm sure you will hear a good report.

I feel certain that his position in charge of POWs would have been very distasteful to him, if he had not been able to ease our burden a little by more humane administration. I've heard reports of some Japanese commanders who were absolute brutes. We are very fortunate to be under this man's command. He used to wear three rows of medal ribbons on state occasions, and it was said that one or two of them had been awarded to him by the British during the First World War. Perhaps that accounts for his sympathetic attitude towards us.

Another thing we noticed about the 'little colonel' was his habit of popping off on a tour of the other camps under his command whenever drastic punishment had to be meted out to the prisoners. I believe he was 'away on business' when four men were shot at Chungkai after trying to escape. We had heard rumours of this shooting further up-country, but it was not until we arrived here that we heard the details. They had been made to dig their own graves; and, refusing to be blindfolded they had died with defiance and contempt on their faces. One is reputed to have laughed in the faces of the men pointing rifles at their breasts.

Well, so much for today's happening. This afternoon's 'yasmi' makes up for this morning's sprucing up and standing around on parade. In addition we have the memory of what must be unique amongst religious services: a characteristically Christian service of remembrance for prisoners of war who died while being forced to build a railway for their enemies. All this by order of the Japanese who are not only the aforesaid enemy, but also a nation with a national religion that is not Christian! Surely the working of the Japanese mind is beyond Western comprehension.

That Christmas is approaching is evident, not only from the preparations being made in the camp, but because the last two or three days have been getting colder. I've had to bring all my resources to bear in order to keep warm at night. Such a statement from one in the tropics must seem rather exaggerated to you at home – and indeed I've no doubt that the thermometer would seem to support you – but we're high in the hills here; maybe a thousand or so feet above sea level; we are also virtually living in the open with clothing that was designed for hot weather.

Love to all

Alan

Note:

This letter finished with a parenthesis (mentioning the grub and going sick). I can't remember why I put this, except it must be something I dared not put down on paper.

Chapter Twenty-Four

The Festive Season Once More

Takanun, Saturday 1 January 1944

My dear Ernest,

Christmas has come and gone once more, and now the New Year is here. The bells of the imagination have rung the death knell of those hopes with which we strengthened ourselves when 1943 was being born. Then, we hoped with unfounded confidence that this Christmas would find us home, or at least at liberty and able to send letters and gifts to those we love at home. Now we look forward into 1944 with those selfsame hopes revived, and stronger than ever. Aye, in spite of all the disappointments our hopes are stronger than ever; for we are martyrs to logic – and logic says that war cannot go on for ever, and at any rate, we are now one year nearer the end than when we welcomed 1943.

Nearly two years have slipped by since we became prisoners: two years with nothing to show for them. Years in which our sole comforts have lain in working out the 'credits' due to us, and in hearing the rumours of good news which we dare not believe, but which no one disbelieves. In our heart of hearts we give them credence, believe me; for although we say otherwise our hearts miss a beat, then work overtime to catch up.

New Year, even more than September 3rd, impresses us with the length of this war and the passage of time. It is with a shock we realise that the war has entered on its fourth year, but almost with panic we realise that we are more than four years older than when there was peace in our time.

I was twenty-one when the war started, and I remember I had that new camera for a twenty-first birthday present. I've hardly used it Ernest, and I'll be twenty-six next birthday! It comes near panic when I think how I had just crossed the threshold of twenty in 1939, but that now I'm nearly thirty!

All the plans I had made have been destroyed, or at least amended. The man of twenty-five visualised then was vastly different from the man I see as I write. One feels scared of going back to pre-war life – the future is so complicated and so be-clouded with fogs of uncertainty that all I can think of is getting back to those I love – I dare not think of anything else.

I suppose you are wondering what's put me in such a bad mood, Ernest. It's certainly nothing in particular; only that I'm always inclined to be morbid at New Year, for the passage of time is emphasised, to my mind, with unkind and persistent relentlessness. One has to remember that 1943 is nothing but history now – the same as 1926. Three hundred and sixty-five days have passed. Fifty-two weeks have gone by. I haven't time to work out the number of hours that have ticked away, second by second, and with so very little to show for them. Such a little has been achieved. I'll certainly not make a good Scotsman, if all the time I say things like that, will I? The poor lads are trying to make merry on practically nothing. In fact they are feeling a little bit sore, I think, because so little has been done for their benefit on their holiday. True, they got hold of some beer or sake (rice wine) last night and tried to make merry on that, but today holds very few prospects.

England beat Scotland at soccer by four goals to one this morning, so they have nothing to crow about there. The tiffin was nothing out of the ordinary – just a so-called Nazi-Goring with peanuts, beans and tinned pork in it. Dinner tonight might be a special effort but I can't say until it comes up.

There's a concert tonight, and if it's anything up to the standard of one Christmas show, it should be worth watching. We had a pantomime called *Babes in Thailand* which was a first-class production worthy of any home stage. It's surprising how such a good show could be made with so few properties. I certainly would like to see it put on in England.

And so Ernest, we try to forget our plight in a day's respite from the work which we know the Japs will find for us to do, thankful for even the smallest mercies.

Love to all

Alan

Chapter Twenty-Five

The Road to Japan

Non Ploduc, 1 June 1944

My dear Ernest,

You'll see by my address that I have moved again. I am now in a transit camp near Bangpong waiting to go to Japan. Since I last wrote, and before we moved here, the Japs kept us occupied with maintenance jobs and cutting wood for the railway.

I believe I mentioned wood cutting before, but I simply must tell you what happened one day when I was put on that job. The normal procedure was for the 'wood party' to fall in and walk down to the hut where the tools were kept. We knew these would be laid in rows in front of the hut: a saw, two or three axes, some iron wedges and a sledgehammer for each party of ten men. Some saws were better than others; so were some axes, and those who had already teamed up would send on ahead their representative to bag the best bag of tools. A mild form of walking race often resulted. The working company I had been placed with was the artillery – made up of the members of several units, as opposed to the Cambs, or the Norfolks which drew their men from one regiment.

The result of this was that I found myself parted from practically all my original comrades, and therefore had to take 'pot luck' as to which party I would work with. On this particular occasion I found myself making up a party with a lot of 'leftovers', some being left over because they had not got a good reputation for work! To make matters worse, we were standing in front of a very inferior looking lot of tools. Being the only NCO in the party, I was put in charge. Not a very enviable position, especially as, in addition to the other troubles, half the gang were fiery little Scots who were disappointed at not being in a Scottish team.

The British Officer, supervising the party, commiserated with us, and told me not to worry if we didn't finish the job. 'Just do as much as you can,' he said.

We went off wondering where to start work. We decided to depart from the usual procedure of felling a large tree, sawing it into half-metre lengths, and splitting these with axes and wedges. We went for the branches left lying around by previous parties. Six went out scouting for good-sized branches while four took turns at the two-handled saw, making sure it was never idle. One of the gang came back with the news that he had found a soft tree. It was only a metre in diameter, but it was soft, and the saw went though it like butter. It helped swell our pile of logs, even if it was not very good for fuel. We all worked with a will – the more so as we saw our stack grow. The four and a half metres were measured out. The metre end piles went up and the space between began to fill up. By just after midday we had finished. Our stack was checked by the Jap overseer, and proud as peacocks, we set off for camp with a jeer on our lips for the other still-toiling gangs who had thought to be back in camp before we had half completed our stint. We were back first, and I still enjoy the memory of that triumph.

Another triumph I still look back on with joy, is the one when a party of us managed to wangle two midday meals. We were sent from our camp to one a little lower down the line to move rice from a store hut. We took two fried rice balls as haversack rations but omitted to mention this fact to the Japs at the other camp. When lunchtime came they provided us with a meal. At the end of the day, when the rice store was half emptied, we made it our business to persuade the Japs to ask for the same party back on the following day to finish the task. We went back, we took two fried rice balls each, and we were provided with lunch again when we got there. Humping sacks of rice is not easy work, but it was worth it to win those extra meals!

At the beginning of February we were given medical inspections by the Japanese. We concluded these were to see if we were fit enough to go to the Land of the Rising Sun. We all seemed to pass, so it couldn't have been a very stiff test.

We left Takanun on 28 February, by steam train, and arrived at Chungkai on March 1st. What a change had taken place since I was last here. There is now a large, well-filled, well-tended cemetery here; and the camp seems to have grown.

It was while we were here that I achieved success as an Anglo-Dutch interpreter. Yes Ernest, it's quite true. The world's worst language scholar turned interpreter. A party of us was called out one night to meet a train full of sick men. We took them off and parked them in huts and proceeded to collect their mess tins for some food. One veteran Dutchman failed to comprehend our English, and there seemed to be a deadlock until I came out with 'Hept U ein blicker?' Out came the mess tin.

We stayed at Chungkai for ten days and then moved to Non Ploduc. And after two and a half months we are still here. There is no work except camp duties for us to do, apart from the odd jobs the Japs dream up. Consequently there is very little going out of camp, and we are thrown on our own resources to keep ourselves occupied.

A group of us, endeavouring to get up a modest programme of entertainment as a much-needed diversion, surprised ourselves by producing a play about a news reporter and a policeman on a trip round London. We visited various well-known places, including the Law Courts, where I had the important part of clerk of the court. The arranging and rehearsing of this show kept us occupied for some time, which was a very good thing; but when the whole thing turned out quite a success I was tickled pink!

I've been able to spend some time carving chessmen from those cigar-shaped toggles you find on tent guyropes. I found several lying around. I feel very pleased with some of the pieces, especially the knights which have a rather jaunty air. What with these chessmen, and the two wood carvings I did at Changi (and which I still have in my bag) I shall have quite a lot to show you when I come home.

We had some sports one day. I had a go at the 220 for 'old time's sake', but I didn't shine.

There is plenty of time for reading and I spend a fair bit of time reading my New Testament (I told you I lost my little Bible, didn't I?). I've covered it with cloth and written 'Enquire within on Everything' on the outside. It's a good motto to remember.

The outstanding memory from the last two and a half months, however, is when about six of us nonconformists got together in an unoccupied hut and held the Lord's

Supper with a simplicity that rivalled biblical days. One produced a biscuit and begged a little tamarind fruit juice in a mug and we used that. True, it was not real wine, but it was all done under difficulties, and we did remember the Lord in 'His Own appointed way'. It was a great uplift to us all, and none of us will forget it.

Unfortunately, we have only been able to arrange this service once, and now there are signs that we may move very soon. I don't know when I shall have another opportunity of writing to you.

When we reach Japan, we are certain to be more restricted. Up until now, with the exception of Selarang, we have known very little of the close confinement one always associated with prisons. 'Iron bars do not a prison make' is a well-known quotation with which I agree. Only at Selarang was I confined to a camp from which I could not have escaped at will. But more powerful than iron bars is the jungle, and far more effective than stone walls is the shape of our faces. I would not stand the slightest chance of passing undetected in this part of the world. I would be recaptured almost immediately, tortured and executed. And if that was not bad enough, my comrades would be punished.

So you see, Ernest, it looks as if I shall have to say 'goodbye' for some time. We are not supposed to have writing materials and I can only write when not observed by the Nips. In Japan I may find this impossible.

Please let everybody read my letter. I send them all my love.

Alan

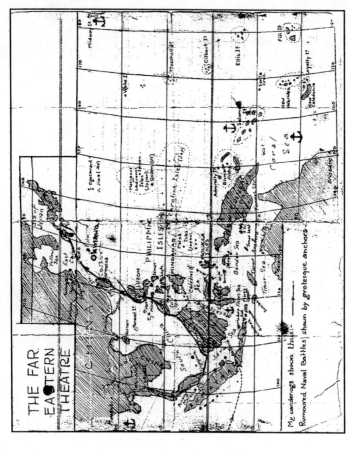

The Far-Eastern Theatre showing my journey to Japan

Chapter Twenty-Six
Alongside the Wharf

Manilla, 22 July 1944

My dear Ernest,

We are alongside the wharf here at Manilla to take on stores. These are being loaded by Philippinos. There's one nearby who is singing with a very fine voice as he works. Perhaps I can give him this letter if I finish it quickly, so let me say briefly what has happened since I last wrote.

We came by train to Singapore, travelling once again in those terrible metal rubber wagons. At the end of that journey my tummy was upset, and it's been that way ever since. We came aboard our boat – the *Asaka Maru* ('Shrine Ship') – 18 June and then anchored offshore for two weeks before sailing for here via the coast of Borneo. They tried to put us all in the hold, but too many of us were overcome by the heat, so the captain gave permission for us to travel as deck cargo.

My pitch is up by the funnel, and when it rains, or the sun shines too brightly I crawl under a lifeboat for what shelter I can find. On top of this, the food is terrible, and I can hardly eat it. All together I feel pretty rotten, and just longing for the end of this journey.

That's all for now, I'm afraid. I hope I have better news to tell next time I write. Please give my love to all.
Alan

PS

I am enclosing a copy I managed to obtain of the address given to us by the top Japanese Officer in Thailand, and given to us before we boarded the ship in Singapore.

ADDRESS & ADMONITION GIVEN ON TRANSPORTATION OF PRISONERS OF WAR
(Given at the Wharf, Singapore, 17th June, 1944)

You are to be transferred from the jurisdiction of POW Camp Thailand to that of Japan where you are to assume labour duty. Since the opening of this Thailand Camp you were diligently carrying out imposed labour duties for more than twenty months, especially you were employed in railway construction in which your discharge of duty attained aimed objective as scheduled, for which we appreciate warmly.

On completion of the above mentioned you are to be transferred to the Holy Land of the Rising Sun where scenery is simply superb. The Empire of Great Japan (proper appellation BEO-Y-YASIMA DAI NIPPON TEIKOKU) is populated with Nationals of up-righteousness, acts of morality brave yet courteous, humane but strictly severe on vices. The proverb most common in use there of 'Even hunter himself will not slay a strayed bird seeking refuge on his lap' will properly explain the attitude and habitude of Japanese sentiments.

The land has four distinct seasons: Spring with abundance of various blossoms, where birds chirp peacefully everywhere; evergreen Summer with cool breezes easing the universe; transparent Autumn skies with clement moon; and with Winter in which snow white washes the whole country, purifying the inhabitants. These are nothing but the image and reflection of His August Imperial Majesty's greatest virtues, of which whole Nationals are bade to follow in Royalty toward the Imperial creation of benevolence etc., etc., to eternal effects.

Therefore, I tell you officers and men – go to Japan with ease of mind and do your imposed duty to perfection. Then I verily tell you that our billion Nationals will be welcoming you to share the Imperial favour with you.

On the other hand, should any one of you still retain conscience of any eneminal Nationals and project, or things be against to the interest of Japan, consequential result must be borne on his own shoulders, however severe or regrettable to all concerned.

I reiterate, believe in Japanese chivalry and go forward in the right way not straying... on proper and mature consideration.

In conclusion I should like to call your attention to take good care of your health, for the sudden change in climatical condition, and wish you the bon accord.

With my blessing for your voyage.

Colonel Nakamura,
Chief of POW Camps, Thailand.
In the year 19th of Shoura.

Chapter Twenty-Seven
A Break in Communications

My original manuscript finished with the letter 'The Festive Season Once More' and dated January 1st, 1944. I did not write any more letters. It may have been because of the cramped conditions on board ship, the fact that we were in transit, or because I had become very weak – and, no doubt, very depressed. I did, however, keep a brief diary of events that I was able to show my brother when I returned home, I feel it quite proper to set down the most important happenings that took place in 1944 and 1945 without pretending they were further letters.

The last three letters were written shortly after release.

June 13th

Arrived at Singapore from Thailand after four or five days in metal freight wagons. 'Never were so many carried so far in so few.'

June 18th

Go on board *Asaka Maru*.

July 4th

Ship sails.

July 16th

Arrive at Manilla. Stay there for three days alongside the Wharf (20–23 July).

August 15th

Shipwrecked after several days enduring a typhoon where I retreated from being 'deck cargo' to joining forces with the coal in the coalbunker. Even the water drips through the deck on to us there. The captain ran the ship aground in a bay on the Southern coast of Formosa.

August 16th

Destroyer comes – stands by and takes us off.

August 17th

Arrive at Formosa – believe the port is called Keelung.

August 20th

Leave Formosa on *Haku San Maru*. One of Japan's most up-to-date liners. *Maru* is the word for 'ship'. *Haku San* means either 'three hundred' or 'Mr Haku'. I believe the former in this case.

Footnote: the *Haku San Maru* came to my notice some months later in a newspaper paragraph where it was stated this ship had left a Asiatic port with a large quantity of Red Cross parcels for POWs in Japan.

August 26th

Arrive at Moji in Japan.

August 28th

Sent in to hospital at Moji – Fukuoka Camp No. 3 suffering from dysentery.

September 29th

Arrive at Ube – the camp in which I am to be kept while I work down the coal mine.

October 7th

Go down the mine for the first time working on the Korgi party (light work).

October 23rd

Start working down the mine concreting a drain in the new under-sea tunnel. This must have been the lowest level of the mine, we had to walk down three flights of steps totalling 1,200 steps altogether. At the end of the shift we had to climb them again. I found it 'murder'.

December 25th

First complete Red Cross given to me – by Father Christmas! (A British Officer with a Russian name and a beard wearing an off-red dressing gown.)

1945

Most of these entries deal with the work I was detailed for – down the mine working on the drain, or cutting coal; working on the surface on various jobs, unloading barges or working on the vegetable garden from 16 April.

References are made to kit allocated by lottery, special notes about food, swaps I did with my cigarette ration. The most interesting items were:

March 27th

First solid 'stool' for months. Good. Up to this time have been subject to the 'squitters' since in Japan. It did not last. We were soon back to the 'squitters' again.

May 3rd (late 2nd)

Whisper that Germany packed in on 28 April.
(This intelligence brought back from the mine by the night shift.)

May 4th (?)

German surrender confirmed by 'the Yank'.
(The Yank was an American Jap on holiday in Japan when their war started and sent to work in the mines. He could not read Japanese and was registered to have a newspaper in English – which he occasionally slipped to one of our lads.)

May 13th

Heard rumours that Germany signed surrender on 8th and that Hitler died on the 1st.

Chapter Twenty-Eight
Everything is 'Sunda'

Ube, Japan, 22 August 1945

My dear Ernest,

At last I feel I have orientated myself sufficiently to utilise a spot of my spare time (of which I have had a fair bit lately) to drop you a line spilling the beans as to what has happened here this last week.

It may be difficult for you to realise just how topsy-turvy I feel mentally now that I know that the war is over. Perhaps you, in dear old England, felt somewhat the same when you heard that Jerry had packed in back in May. But whatever you felt then could not be nearly as disturbing as all this has felt to me; for not only have I been a fretting prisoner, longing for my release, but I have become mentally unbalanced to a certain extent – as I believe I explained in a previous letter.

I suppose you'll be finding scholastic errors in every line of this letter – being a schoolmaster – but I must claim that as proof of just how 'skew-wiff' my brain box is.

Realising how probable a mental hiatus (that's a good word anyhow, and should please you) was, I jotted down the events of this last week day by day, so that I could keep my facts as accurate as possible. If I give you a day by day account from these notes, enlarging on them where necessary, I think you will get the clearest picture I can paint of these momentous days.

Everything outside the camp seems so strange and silent. Everything is at a standstill. In fact all is a fulfilment of the phrase that has run through my mind for the last fortnight – a corruption of the title of a book in our library called *Everything is Thunder*, which I believe is well known as a recent 'hit': a phrase that runs, 'Everything is Sunda'. It's a poor joke if one has to explain it, I know, but in this case the phrase has so haunted me that I am risking your contempt and mentioning it together with the explanation that 'Sunda' is Jap for 'finish' or 'end'. It's one of those pleasant words we like to hear down the pit – like 'yasmi' (rest) and 'Mishi' (grub).

August 15th

Work as per detail on camp air raid shelter (working on a shift basis of twenty minutes 'on top', twenty minutes 'down the hole' and twenty minutes rest). During the morning sirens go and up goes the red and white flag. To our disgust we did not knock off and go down the other shelter (we were working on a new deep shelter). Observers notice both guardroom and office are very quiet and seem deserted, while all of us could hear loud speakers working overtime. Observers also report that what Nips are around (including 'the Wing') look very glum. (The Wing, by the way, is the one armed Jap interpreter, who is not liked by anybody.)

The 'all-clear' went about midday. The afternoon miners paraded late and quickly fell out again, being told 'Yama ni'. (Mine, no.) The explanation given was that the electric supply had failed.

The morning shift miners arrive back in camp early, followed by the 'Korgi' men (light surface workers).

By this time we are convinced something is seriously wrong, and when one lad, who had been on Korgi, told us that Nip boys they passed had raised their hands as in surrender, and said 'Nippon', we found it hard not to think optimistically.

I opened a tin of butter (put away for Eileen's birthday on the 20th) on the strength of my wishful thinking; all the time telling myself and others that whatever has happened, it is not the end of the war.

August 16th

Worked on air raid shelter again – most disgusting, as apart from the usual camp fatigues we were the only ones working. No mine, korgi, or nothing! Routine was the same as yesterday – three shifts – but if anything, progress was slower. The end of the job was in sight however, so we speeded up after tiffin to finish early. When nearly done the Nip commandant came and knocked us off. We had the last laugh however, for we got our working bonus of seventy grammes of rice.

Everywhere very quiet – no raid warning since midday yesterday. Hopes rise higher and higher, especially when we had our particulars taken for reorganisation purposes.

Finished off bones – about a week ago a load of bones came into the cookhouse. After the cooks had finished stewing them they were carefully divided between the huts. Each hut divided them carefully into sufficient portions and drew lots for each man. I have *eaten* all mine after days of soaking.

August 17th

Passed a bad night – due no doubt to the combined effects of last night's coffee and the bugs, which found me although I slept on a couple of forms to avoid them.

Had a shave with a new blade – still on the strength of high hopes.

Hopes justified, as just after 9 a.m. official announcement was made that the 'war is over'. We restrained our cheers by urgent request although we could clearly hear No. 5 hut cheering.

Washed British KD clothing (in anticipation of move, when I want to wear it). While doing so volunteers were called for to get Red Cross stores from the mine. Did not go because in the middle of washing clothes; but got clamped for fatigue of emptying rubbish bin into the air raid shelter I had just helped to dig. Dumped rubbish in small shelter more conveniently placed, dumping only the surplus in the big pit. It seemed all wrong filling in shelters, but we are not used to peace yet.

Rations cut down to 'yasmi-day' level (about 360 grammes of rice).

In draw for extra Red Cross articles, succeeded in getting only sugar, soap and cigarettes – not very fortunate.

August 18th

Spent another bad night on the forms – bugs very hungry.

Had medical history recorded and particulars of pay taken in the morning. Handed in mining boots. Glad to see the back of these rubber-soled canvas boots that fasten up behind the heel. They were either too small or far too big in size and not at all comfortable.

In afternoon, repair socks (in anticipation of boots).

Toffee issued from the cookhouse – not enough for me though.

Part 1 Orders published – we will have to get back into the habit of looking at the notice-board.

Spent some time getting organised for a move in the near future, throwing out a lot of junk that I had accumulated.

August 19th (Sunday)

Off the mark early with fatigues this morning – it's wonderful how the fatigues crop up now we are under our own officers. We had to clear up round our huts before breakfast as some big-pot Nips were expected.

During the day collect several fatigues, and thinking there was something 'fishy' about it, went to see Mr James after thanksgiving service. Discovered I was on punishment fatigues because I did not volunteer to go down the pit yesterday – collected fatigues without a chance to say anything in my defence and on false information from 'Q' Gledow.

Found the thanksgiving service very touching. To avoid the risk of trouble with the civilians we did not sing the hymns. Perhaps that was just as well, for when we recited *Oh God our Help in Ages Past* I was not the only one with tears in my eyes. We also recited the National Anthem. It's strange how hard it is to remember the words when you are not singing the tune.

Between fatigues, I made a watch strap out of a piece of mining belt. Watches, etc. have come out of pound now and may be flashed around.

August 20th (Eileen's Birthday)

Last night I slept out in the open and had a good night's rest – I've been foolish not to sleep out earlier. In the afternoon, went down the pit to fetch medical supplies and clothing. I hope that's the last time I see this pit.

Spent spare time making rank badge for wrist – have to wear our rank now; we're in the British Army.

Celebrated today with special private menu made up from Red Cross goods, and by reading through Eileen's letters. Stuck Eileen's photograph up in a window frame. Felt nice and sentimental.

Today was a red letter day as the Nips officially told us that the war was over, and tonight the orders regarding blackout were lifted.

On orders, a notice was published, stating that 'men will shave, and on Roll Call will parade properly dressed.' (British Army again.) Evening roll call tonight was in English fashion. We were so used to the Nip method, that we make a real mess of it.

After roll call, there was a draw for articles sent by the Red Cross but not allowed in our possession by the Nips (scissors, combs, etc.). Drew a comb.

Tonight, lights stream unhindered from the windows.

August 21st

Surprisingly my watch seems to be behaving satisfactorily – all the time it's been one of the very few watches in the camp; it's been very temperamental. Now there are lots of watches about, it goes. Competition must have put it on its 'metal'.

In spare time repair a bag and made new rank arm badge.

'Basic Ration' of rice increased from 360 to 710 grammes (please remember there are 435 grammes in a pound). There was rice for breakfast, tiffin *and* dinner. The evening stew was thick enough to stand a spoon up in – I did.

August 22nd

Today, kicked off with a visit to the library after breakfast where I took out a book of reminiscences by a journalist – looks like proving an interesting and entertaining volume. The officers were paid some money outstanding to them, this morning. Soon they were telling how the Nip medical sergeant had said they could use the money as 'benjo paper', when they complained there was nothing to spend it on. It shows what he thinks about his country's financial position at the moment.

Somehow or other the time dragged heavily today although I made some notes and succeeded in roasting some beans I had. I proceeded to 'scoff' them immediately.

Experimented with cheese and jam on rice, and found myself undecided whether it was worth trying again.

Had a chance of spending sixty cents on some 'cachus' of a vague mentholated nature. Jumped at the chance although it was nothing more than a waste of cash.

Medical note – yellow colour of urine. Previously colourless. Suggests we are getting a better supply of vitamins.

And that, Ernest, gives you some idea of my first week since the curtain was rung down on this war. Of course, there is still a lot of chin-wagging and round table conferences to be got through; crowds of agreements and decisions to be reached, as well as an innumerable variety of things to be arranged and organised – notably the transportation of POWs to their natural surroundings – but in spite of these details, the major issue of fighting is over, I believe. As I said before 'Everything is Sunda', and 'Oh Boy!' am I looking forward to coming home! The thought that soon home will be not merely a possibility, but a reality, keeps coming over me in waves now and then, and knocking me all of a heap with emotion. I very much doubt if the shores of dear old England will remain visible to my eyes for very long when we first sight them, for I suspect that a sentimental streak in me will have full play and along with many others I shall be overcome by emotion. It will be worth it however.

I can't say I'm impatient to get home though. I've been away so long that I just can't grasp a homecoming as a thing of the near future. In fact, I've set my heart on coming home via America, if possible even if it means waiting two or three months longer before I see you all again. I hope this doesn't sound unloving and selfish. I must pull up my socks (which are full of holes) and start trying to adjust myself to face a meeting.

It's taken me two or three sessions to write all this, Ernest, and I'm tired of writing now. Anyhow, there's enough here to be going on with, so I'll close with love and kisses all round.

Stop Press:

Had visitors tonight from HQ Camp at Hiroshima. Two Nips on a tour, checking up on the camps in the group. One of them had been educated at Cambridge and Mr James, our interpreter (by virtue of having learned and remembered more Japanese than anybody else in the camp) said it was strange to hear perfect college English spoken by one of these people.

In answer to questions, which they invited, they said that in their opinion our stay here will be from seven to ten days longer. Let's hope that is not an underestimate. They hold out no hopes of mail or newspapers for us, and owing to serious disruption, we can't send you cables.

They reckon it unlikely that we will get any more Red Cross parcels – bad, that, very!

They also said that negotiations for peace are going on in Manilla, which shows us which way the victory has gone. (We, of course, don't know that officially as yet, but if the Nips have to go to the Yanks' home ground for talks, it leaves little room for doubt, does it?)

There was also talk of European grub soon – an item of news that certainly lies very near our hearts.

I think you will agree that gives us something to dream about tonight – an experiment I think I'll try and put into operation now. So, goodnight Ernest, and pleasant dreams.
Alan

Afterthought
(Commonly called 'Epilogue')

On reading this manuscript again after fifty years, I am impressed by many things I have left out – things that are still clear in my memory, and that I have often recounted; but few of which, upon reflection, would have found their way into letters to my brother written in such a lighthearted vein in order to combat the anxiety felt by loved ones at home for my safety and well-being.

For instance, what was the point of writing about the fears we had on capitulation that the Japs would massacre the lot of us? Or at least, subject us to humiliating treatment from which we might never be able to recover?

Then there was the first sight I had of a Japanese soldier. It was as we were trudging from Singapore out to Changi. Every so often there was a soldier with a rifle making sure we were keeping to the prescribed route. I remember wondering how I should look. Dejected, beaten and humiliated, or unbowed and still defiant? After all, we were British soldiers. I did not like the look of that rifle and opted for unbowed, but undefiant!

We were expected to conform to Japanese ideas of discipline when we got to Changi. Our officers were told to take off their rank badges from their shoulders and wear a single pip on their breast pocket. We were told to salute Japanese sentries on guard duty. That came hard if he was a half-pint sized third-class private. Some hot-heads refused to do so and were beaten up. After all, the Japs had to salute as well.

We quickly learned the Japs despised us for surrendering. I suppose we should have committed hara-kiri! My original manuscript says nothing of the journey from Singapore to Siam, so shortly after I arrived home I added the chapter 'Change of Address' to fill the gap. I also added the chapter 'Once I Built A Railroad'. The last chapter 'Everything is Sunda' is genuine, but I felt 'The Road to Japan' and 'Alongside the Wharf' needed to be added. The summary of the sea journey and time spent in Japan are recent additions.

There were some vivid memories which would have been out of place in these letters to my brother.

For example, the discussions I had with various comrades about writing and publishing books. I remember showing part of what I had written to Mac. He certainly had more idea than I had for he said my language was not strong enough. Writing of the illness among our men he counselled I should have said the ulcers and other diseases we were suffering from were due to 'starvation'. That sounded rather dramatic to me at the time as, way up in the jungle, we were eating better than at any other time. We were at the camp where the half-dead pigs were being brought ashore from the river boats. Many were too far gone to survive and had to be killed – and eaten in our camp – to the loss of other camps up the line.

Poor Mac! I remember him saying, to my surprise for he did not seem particularly religious, 'When this war is over the first thing I am going to do is to go down on my knees and thank God.' I heard a vague rumour that he did not survive.

Sitting round in the heat after the day's work we had nothing much to do except talk; there was very little light. If you were lucky there might be a home-made lamp made with a piece of string dipped in oil. Some times there might be a candle. Mostly we talked about food, and the lavish, bilious-attack provoking dishes we would demand when we got home. On one occasion it was about the medals we would be entitled to when the war was over. I think I managed to work out I might get eight – after all, I had been with the BEF in France in 1940; and then there was the Irish Campaign in 1941 when I was having a whale of a time in Northern Ireland; and so on. I ended up with only three – the two everybody got, plus the star for the Far East Campaign – and that had a yellow streak down the middle of it! Deserved, I suppose, as we did run away down Malaya!

I remember experimenting in making candles, I cannot remember where the candles came from but I collected up the precious wax droppings, splitting a hollow bamboo, fastening a string between two joints to keep it in the middle, and filling it with melted wax. I had a nice six-inch candle about three-quarters of an inch in diameter. It burnt a treat, but was finished in about a minute flat. I had got it wrong somewhere. I think I should have kept dipping the wick in melted wax.

I also made a spoon out of an aluminium soap dish. The one I made out of the lid was a disaster. I cut it out to the conventional shape of a rounded bowl, then a narrow neck gradually widening to the handle. Of course, it was too weak. The second effort was a real success being modelled on the principle of the oriental design where there is no neck and a crease down the handle giving added strength. I still have it as a souvenir.

The nearest I came to the suicidal action of hitting a Japanese guard was when working on the Chungkai quarries. Rocks and rubble scraped from the cliff face were loaded onto two little trucks and wheeled down a rickety railway line to where they could be tipped to help make the adjoining embankment. There, two men would heave the truck sideways to empty it down the slope. If you were not careful you could trap your fingers when the body inevitably slid down the axle against the wheels. That is exactly what my companion did, nearly cutting off his fingers. Taramoto, the Jap officer was standing there watching his distress. Callously he looked at the injured hand, then indicated he should carry on working. I felt like hitting him. He was one of the brutal type.

I shall never forget the death of 'Smiler' Lorriman when we were living in tents up near the Burma border. He slept next to me and went down with cerebral malaria. In the middle of the night he was obviously very ill, so we sent for the MO. Seeing our hostile looks (we were sure the officers were not pulling their weight), he explained he was going to use a syringe to draw off fluid from his spine to ease the convulsions. I was glad when a little later he sent a stretcher to take him elsewhere. He died before morning and we buried him in a small clearing in the jungle where there were half a dozen other graves. No coffin: he was just wrapped in rice sacks.

Life was not all doom and gloom, however. All the time we were in Thailand we never felt we were in prison. Sometimes there was not even a flimsy bamboo fence round us as a token of how far we were allowed to wander. There is a lot of bamboo in the jungle. We collected it for constructing huts and for firewood, among other things. I remember going out, all alone, to collect firewood; dressed only in a pair of shorts and a hat, with broken down plimsoles on my feet that threatened to slip off every few steps, and singing at the top of my voice. It was a chorus I learnt in Bible class: 'Safe am I in the hollow of His hand. Sheltered o'er in His Love for evermore.'

When we left Siam to go to Japan I was unable to write many 'letters'. Survival was becoming too serious a business, and we had virtually no privacy. I had to content myself with short notes, many of which were worked into the added letters I have already mentioned.

We journeyed from Singapore in a cargo ship named, I believe, the *Asaka Maru*. If I had been well enough (I had started with dysentery), and had the privacy, I would probably have written that the ship had a plaque saying it was built in Britain on a date before the First World War. Also, I might have said how before they could pack us all down in the hold men began fainting, and eventually the Captain gave permission for those who wanted to sleep on deck, which I did. I chose a spot in the shelter of a lifeboat. We soon pulled away from the quay, but then found ourselves stuck offshore for a fortnight before we started our voyage. When we did go we travelled up the north coast of Borneo, anchoring for a while off Mirri, which appeared to have a lot of oil rigs dotted about the hills.

I am sure I would have mentioned how 'toilet facilities' were accomplished by clambering over the rail of the ship into a large wooden box lashed to the side. There was a hole in the bottom through which you could see water rushing by. Then you had to clamber back on board, which was rather unnerving when there was much of a swell.

The Japanese guard escorting us held a daily parade. They would line up at the rail and recite something which we presumed was an oath of loyalty to the Emperor. Of course, we put our own interpretation on it: 'You are a mighty emperor. I'm sorry I didn't die for you today, but I will try to die for you tomorrow' etc., etc.

One of the highlights of that voyage (and there weren't many) was when the guard lined up one evening facing out to sea towards their equivalent to Mecca when they suddenly realised they were facing the wrong way. Confusion, break ranks, line up on the other side of the ship and start again.

One of the lowest points of my existence was when I saw my kit bag washed overboard in some rough weather. It contained my wood carvings which I had carried all round Thailand. Fortunately my closest treasures, kept in a sponge-bag, were still on deck.

We got caught in a typhoon, disastrous when you are travelling as deck cargo so I crawled into the coal bunker and lay on the coal. I was out of the storm, but water kept dripping on to me through leaks in the deck, making life even more unpleasant.

It was on this ship I collapsed. I don't remember too much about it, but know I came to the conclusion the stiff upper lip was not doing any good, and if one became a casualty, somebody would do something about it.

The typhoon evidently made the *Asaka Maru* spring a leak in a more strategic place than the deck, for the captain decided to run aground in a little bay at the south end of Formosa, or Taiwan as it is now called. We stuck there till a destroyer came by and took us all off in rowing boats. The Japanese sailors did very well in spite of the fact I was supposed to help with the rowing.

Once on board the destroyer we were taken to a port on the north of the island. I still remember the thrill as (travelling as deck cargo once more) the destroyer literally bounded over the waves.

We were transferred to a modern passenger ship – there were civilians on it so we were battened down below decks.

It was the *Haku San Maru* – either 'Mr Haku ship' or 'Ship 300', by my translation. Although a modern ship the toilets were definitely designed for native use – no seats.

While battened down below hatches we heard destroyers dropping depth charges. One of the most frightening moments of my life. Depth charges meant American submarines. That meant torpedoes. That meant sinking ships and we were caught like rats in a trap.

We were allowed up on deck for brief spells at night. I remember seeing a large 'whaler' in the convoy. The next night it had disappeared.

On deck for a breather one night we saw a ship on fire. A destroyer was standing by playing a searchlight over the waters – looking for survivors.

It was on 'No. 300 ship' I suffered from loss of memory. It was so strange for I remembered it vividly. Being crowded we had only enough deck space to lie down on. Whenever I left mine 'to go to benjo', which was frequently, I could never find my way back again, and would wander round and round the cargo space until I found something I recognised.

I believe this was one of the last convoys to get through to Japan. When I came off 'No. 300' in September 1944 I went straight into hospital with dysentery and malaria, while the rest of the party went on to their destination.

I joined them a month later, travelling with another prisoner under escort among all the civilians. I thought the trains very good, and especially a major station where we changed trains. Civilians were all over the place, but my outstanding memory was of a party of Japanese servicemen, probably Navy, looking smart in their while uniforms and carrying urns with the ashes of their dead comrades.

The scenery reminded me of the GWR line in South Devon.

And so we came to the Ube, on Japan's main island facing the Inland Sea. The men in the camp were working down a coalmine, appropriately named 'Mountain Under the Sea' if I remember the translation aright. Very appropriate as some of the galleries went out under the sea. I did light work around the camp at first, then worked on a garden we were making a good walk away from the camp.

After that I ended up working down the mine, mostly concreting a drain in a new tunnel we reached by descending 1,200 steps, and up which we had to trudge at the end of the shift! Some of the time I was put on cutting coal from the face and flinging it on to a conveyor belt. None of this was I able to write in the form of rather light-hearted letters to my brother – and indeed much of it I would have deliberately left out. It would not have had an authentic sound to it, and anyway it would not have been honest. Much better to let my brief notes speak for themselves.

As I look back after fifty years many other memories come to mind. Such as the time I was left on my own down the coal mine with half-a-dozen women doing some light work. Evidently we got on famously for they kept exclaiming 'Yoorashee!' which I believe meant something like 'Very good!' or 'Well done!' – even though I could not have been working very hard.

On another occasion down the mine I walked beside our Japanese 'contact' who passed the English version newspaper to certain detailed fellow POWs. He was registered to receive it because he could not read Japanese. In a rich American accent he told me how the Japs had no hope of winning this war.

Right at the end – when the Japs had surrendered and we were wondering what would happen next, I volunteered to help sew together 'silk' from red, white and blue parachute canopies to make a Union Jack we could fly in the camp. Our sewing was not all that good, and the thread we used was even worse; and I am convinced it would have fallen to bits the first time we flew it. We never tried to fly it but it was used once – as a shroud to bury that lad so addicted to smoking that he gave his food away for cigarettes. How sad! To endure three and a half years in prison camps and then to die just when freedom came!

'And were there any outstanding memories of those days?' you ask.

The most chilling memories must be the fear of what the Japs might do to us when we capitulated at Singapore. And again, what would be our guards' reaction when they were told they had lost the war. Would they, instead of committing hara-kiri in the approved way decide we could be slaughtered instead? There was the horrific four-day journey from Singapore to Thailand crammed into all metal wagons designed for transporting raw rubber; and the same journey in the opposite direction about sixteen months later. In Thailand I remember travelling in the back of an Army truck along a very bumpy makeshift road while we were building that infamous 'railway of death'. The driver went far too fast for comfort and we were bounced about like dice about to be thrown out on to the Ludo board. We felt we were going to be thrown out of the truck in the same way. I confess it drove me to pray very hard for preservation.

As I also did when battoned down below decks somewhere between Formosa and Japan, and I could hear the Japanese destroyers dropping depth charges to kill US submarines threatening our convoy.

Crammed into huts in Ube at the top of the coal mine where we were working, with our nerves all a-jangle, it was virtually impossible to say any idle pleasantry without somebody taking offence. A forced laugh often helped to keep tempers calm. No wonder I arrived home with a near-hysterical laugh!

'But were there any highlights you fondly remember?' you may ask.

Yes. There were cherished moments spent in the company of men spiritually oriented like myself. There was that time when half a dozen of us were able to hold an informal communion service often referred to as the Lord's Supper.

On another occasion, in Takanun, up among the mountains near the Burmese border, when four of us got together in a quiet corner and I reminded the others of Psalm 125 verse 2, which reads 'As the mountains are round about Jerusalem...' – I paused there and substituted 'Takanun' for 'Jerusalem', and continued '...so the Lord is round about his people from henceforth even for ever.'

Apart from such moments, the highlights I remember were when we got together a choir and sang in harmony; sometimes simple hymns or carols, sometimes a song for one of the shows got up to entertain others in the camp, sometimes even classical pieces like Offenbach's *Barcarole*. Yes, singing in harmony. To conclude I return to the incident when sheltering in the coal bunker on the tramp ship during the typhoon. It is one of my most vivid memories. I was free from the wind but damp and miserable, but I kept repeating to myself a verse from a booklet called 'Every Day', with thoughts for each day of the month. It went like this:

> God is with thee! It matters not
> If none beside remain,
> He knows the sadness of thy lot
> And turns thy loss to gain –
> Works through the things that seem amiss
> External good for thee.
> And leads thee by such ways as this
> His perfect love to see.

I know it's true, for it helped!

As the Mountains are Round about Takanun

*illustrated by Dr Robert Handie in his book
'The Burmas Siam Railway'*

Part Two

Upon Release

The diary kept from VJ Day to the time when we boarded the hospital ship *Consolation* to leave Japan. The first week is recorded in the last letter in *Chained Mail*, which was written on the journey home.

The sign of the mining company we worked for in Ube. It faced the Inland Sea and was about seventy miles from

Hiroshima and about a hundred miles from Nagasaki. We wore this sign on the back of our flimsy mining jackets. 'Yama' means 'mine' in Japanese and is the same word as for 'mountain'. 'Mountain Under the Sea' is, I believe, the name of the mining company. The use of Nippon (or Nip) for Japan (or Jap) may be confusing, but seems to be a matter of taste. I never found out which they preferred.

Apparently this is how my name looks in Japanese. It is a tracing from the label I had to wear in my hat in Thailand. A Nip guard once called me by name after reading it.

> **ALL RUBBISH WILL BE**
>
> **DEPOSITED IN THE AIR RAID**
>
> **SHELTER**

This notice was chalked on a board propped up near the shelter. What could be greater proof of the fact the war was over?

August 23rd

Duty Platoon today. In the morning moved the Nip office out of camp. Managed to scrounge half a dozen pencils and some paper. In the afternoon was put in charge of wood fatigue and made two trips with barrow.

In other ways quite a red letter day as we had issues of salt, curry, tea and tobacco (thirty sen worth which I sold to George for fifty vitamin pills which he said someone had been about to throw away).

Music on the square during the evening – gramophone records.

August 24th

Mess orderly – a job we don't mind doing these days. Pretend to show my influence with the cooks (or the power of my lucky star) by bringing in a meat stew – the first proper one since we came to Japan.

Called out on fatigue to go down the mine to fetch clothing. Don mining kit for the last time, I hope. Back late for tiffin so do not do mess orderly job. Scrounged a useful wad of writing paper while underground.

Today's highlight was the news that aircraft are expected over tomorrow to drop food and messages, and we must prepare identification marks in the form of large 'POW's to facilitate location of the camp.

Went on bathing parade in the afternoon, but finding a comfy spot in the shade, sat down and jotted notes. The real idea of going on this parade was to get out of the camp.

Two draws today. In one I won the right to buy a pair of socks for fifty sen. I had no luck in the other which was for Red Cross blankets lately used in the hospital.

August 25th

Another good night's sleep.

Today, started on increased rations – from 710 grammes to 1,450 grammes. Made a proper pig of myself and blew myself out as tight as a drum each meal.

Attended choir practice, organised to prepare for the service tomorrow, when it has been decided to have as much of it sung as possible.

Bathing parade again this afternoon. Took towel and book but neither bathed nor read. Spent time jotting down notes. It was nice to get away from the camp and away from the flies. (This passion for jotting down notes arose from the dream-like quality of the existence at this time. I felt I could never remember the details or recapture the atmosphere unless I made notes on the spot.)

At 1 p.m. we had a parade to show off our footwear and Nip shirts. Afterwards I washed the shirt ready for handing in. Had issued a winter shirt which I hope does not signify we will be staying here that long. Also issued an extremely frail hand towel. What I want to see is some new footwear.

For tea I took more than I could eat and had to put some of my beans away for later. After Roll Call heard rice-balls were being given away at the cookhouse. Went to investigate and eventually came away with a big one weighing well over 200 grammes and made of rice and beans. I estimate I consumed 1,800 grammes of rice (or somewhat over 4 pounds dry weight). We also had a meat stew.

The beans I had put by I eventually consumed at 1 a.m. when disturbed by a spot of rain and had slept off most of the uncomfortable feeling within.

Disappointment reigned in the camp tonight as no aircraft have turned up. Popular opinion thinks food was going to be dropped.

August 26th

A disturbed night because of rain. Awake from 12 to 3 a.m. wondering which was the lesser of the two evils – the rain or the bugs. Decided in favour of the rain. In the morning we had another choir practice. While waiting for it to begin, went to the MI Room and weighed myself. Turned the scale at 54.8 kilos. When last weighed on the 11th I turned the scale at 50.6 kilos. This shows an increase of four kilos, or about nine pounds.

The morning produced a fair spot of rain, but the afternoon cleared up sufficiently to make the bathing parade enjoyable. We tried a different spot today which meant a longer walk – all to the good in my opinion. I did not take a towel this time, relying on my notebook and pencil to pass the time.

Another day of 'big eats'. For tiffin we had a lump of pork and no stew. I opened my butter, and made it a pleasant meal. Tea was a vegetable hash which was very nice.

The aircraft we had been expecting all day again didn't turn up so the church service, which had been delayed because of possible interruption, was eventually held after dark at 8 o'clock with the aid of flood lighting. A small but appreciative group gathered and the service was said to be a confirmation of our thanksgiving service last Sunday. The hymn, 'All good gifts around us are sent from heaven above' was not included in the service so the aerobatics we had been expecting would have been out of place. I was not very impressed with the service until in conclusion we sang the national anthem – the first time for years – when the reality of our deliverance struck me afresh.

August 27th

A shower of rain in the night drove me inside. On looking at my bed space I noticed it was alive with bugs so decided to sleep in the passage, but the little wretches still found me. Net result, rather a bad night.

The rain was forerunner of a typhoon which raged all day, only dying down when night came. Naturally it kept us indoors. We were all right in the morning because the wind was driving the rain against the opposite side of the hut – much to the discomfort of those living there: but in the afternoon the wind veered right round and we got the full force on our side. The glass had been taken out as air raid precautions and the rain beat in a treat. We had a delightful time collecting panes of glass and shoving them in the frames.

About 5.30 a.m. we had heard a plane fly over very low. We wondered if it was the plane to drop supplies, but the visibility was far too poor for that.

In the morning had a haircut. Told the barber 'short back and sides' and meant it. None of your clippers all over the top! The rest of the time I wrote and tried making a purse in anticipation of having a few dimes and nickels to play with soon. I used a piece of KD cloth and some machine belting obviously from the 'Yama', and used as a battery shield on a mining belt.

The typhoon did quite a lot of damage in the camp. Not only did the rain drive in but it also poured in through the roof in some places. Quite a stretch of the boundary fence was laid flat while in other places it was tottering perilously. The electricity wires were brought down and we went to bed in the dark, with a general warning ringing in our ears that the typhoon might make the sea rise abnormally and cause damage. Zero hour was 10 p.m. We had to be on the lookout to skip for our lives. All of which sounded very thrilling.

LETTER FROM THE SWISS CONSULATE – TOKYO
(Received 09.20 hours 28 August 1945)

To be communicated to the POW by the camp representative.
To the Prisoners of War.

'The hour of your liberation has come.'

Representatives of the Protective Powers, Switzerland (Americans, British, Australians etc.) – Sweden (Nederlands etc.) and the undersigned are in touch with the Allied High Command and will assist the Japanese Authorities in your evacuation.

A speedy and comfortable evacuation can only be assured if you collaborate and maintain order to the last.

For this reason you are requested to follow the instructions of your CAMP REPRESENTATIVES, who will be in contact with us, and will receive all the necessary information.

Therefore please be patient and do not create any disturbance which might delay your evacuation.

Japan should see you leave with all your honour and dignity.

The Delegate of the International Red Cross Committee.
(signed) FRITZ W. BULFINGER
Fuchu-machi. August 27, 1945, 09.00 hours

THE INSTRUCTIONS RECEIVED ALONG WITH THE SWISS CONSUL'S LETTER

The JAPANESE Government has surrendered.

You will be evacuated by ALLIED NATION'S forces as soon as possible. Until that time, your present supplies will be augmented by airdrop of US food, clothing and medicines. The first drop of these items will arrive within one (1) or two (2) hours. Clothing will be dropped in standard packs of 50 or 500 men. Bundles markings contents and allowances per man are as follows.

Contents and allowances per man:

Undershirt	2	Kit sewing	1
Socks (pr)	2	Soap toilet	1
Shirt	1	Razor	1
Trousers	1	Blades Razor	1
Jacket (field)	1	Powder insecticide	1
Belt webb waist	1	Brush tooth	1
Shoes (pr)	1	Paste tooth	1
Drawers	2	Laces shoe	1
Handkerchiefs	3	Comb	1
Cap HBT	1	Shaving cream	1
Towel	1		

There will be instructions with the food and medicines for their use and distribution.

<u>CAUTION</u>   DO NOT OVEREAT OR
OVERMEDICATE
FOLLOW DIRECTIONS

August 28th

Another disturbed night. Gallantly 'got down to it' on my bed space, hoping I was too tired to worry about the bugs – I wasn't; and after an hour of bug-squashing I looked for a fresh billet. I found it on the wash bench, after which I got a fair bit of sleep. Just as well, for I'm sure my blankets would have been soaked in blood by morning if I had remained inside.

Today proved bright and sunny. The storm had cleared the air a treat.

In the morning a letter was received from the Swiss Consulate with instructions, stating that the hour of our liberation had come, and that supplies would be air-dropped. It was put on the notice-board along with a note that further information would be given out on a special parade called for 13.00 hours. Later in the morning paraded for leather boots, and received a pair size 117 Nip army boots. They look quite good stuff and – oh boy! – they fit me a treat! What I've been pining for has been a pair of boots!

The special parade was never held, however. Just before one o'clock bomber aircraft appeared low over the camp and started dropping supplies by parachute. The planes (some lads said they were B29s but they had no more idea than me) had the white star on the fuselage and carried the letter 'T' on the tail. On the wings was clearly painted 'PW Supplies'.

As the planes came over the camp we all waved furiously; and suddenly I discovered I was cheering along with the rest. Why, I don't know, for it was obvious the pilot could not hear us.

Altogether seven runs were made, each dropping about a dozen chutes with bundles attached. The bundles were nothing more than large oil-drums, sometimes two welded together and hurriedly stuffed with goodies. It all seemed very badly done for nearly half the drums broke away from their chutes and came down a lovely wallop. Some even burst open in mid-air and scattered all their contents before they landed.

Some of the containers had crashed onto houses, absolutely wrecking them; and I understand three persons were killed (a later report suggested they were only badly injured).

We were filled with excitement to such an extent that I actually volunteered to go out of camp to collect the stuff that had fallen. What a mess some of them were! A considerable portion of the goods were wasted by bursting open. This waste seemed terrible to me. For so long now I have been carefully avoiding waste of any description that to see food stuff scattered around, and spoiled beyond hope of use appeared criminal to me. I gathered up odd lumps of soap lying about and when I returned to the camp I had a ball of soap like an outsized riceball, which I dutifully handed into the stores.

The local GPO received a direct hit and a liberal supply of cocoa tinted the wall a delightful colour. Although the wall was of concrete the canister crashed right through and landed near the counter where they dispense the postage stamps. No stamps were in evidence so I was not tempted to help myself – which, I confess, I would have found hard to resist if I had seen any.

No time was wasted in lobbing the stuff out to us. The food, of course, was given in to the cookhouse, and they got busy with tin openers on the damaged cans right away. We had a good stew for the evening meal.

Whether the electric cables were repaired after the storm I cannot say, for the falling canisters had brought more wires down, so we were left in darkness once again. We had a lamp from the mine, however, which proved very useful as the cooks got cracking and dished out a drink of cocoa. That should help me to sleep tonight.

I've made a lot of trips to the latrine today, but mostly it was wind that had formed in my stomach and I felt it wise to take precautions over getting rid of it. I've had the 'squitters' (a more expressive word and easier to spell than 'diarrhoea') for so long now that it comes like second nature.

During the afternoon and evening we had quite a lot of kit issued to us.

When we ran out of back-fastening rubber plimsoles to wear down the mine the Japanese issued us with these 'straws' (so called because that is what they were made of). Some men had to work down the mine with nothing else on their feet. Fortunately my plimsoles lasted long enough for me never to need these.

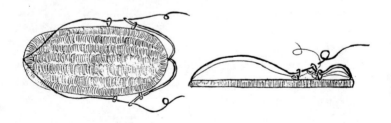

Straws
Issued for working down the mine to those whose rubber plimsoles wore out

August 29th

The main features of the day were (a) the issuing of kit etc. – every hour or so something new was brought into the hut for distribution; and (b) the smaller meals that were dished out. We had much less rice today, but we had stews such as we have not seen for years. We even had sweet courses to follow. I prefer it this way. I would have eaten more if I could have got it, but I am glad I couldn't. I just cannot resist overeating yet, if the food is there to eat. There were issues of cocoa in mid-morning and also as a night cap. Never have we lived so luxuriously.

In the afternoon I went on bathing parade (still with no intention of bathing) and explored a lighthouse on the end of the jetty. Climbing up to the lantern I was surprised to find the lamp used was only three hundred watts on a hundred volt circuit. The recent typhoon did plenty of damage here, making a real mess of some concrete steps used by the bathers last time we came out. There was also a boat lifted high and dry on to the beach.

The Japs very generously gave us some soap and toilet paper – things we longed for a couple of weeks ago, but which, in these times of plenty, seem rather ridiculous.

For the evening meal – dumplings in stew.

August 30th

Just after breakfast we had the excitement of seeing planes circling round with cargo doors open, and looking for all the world as if they were going to give us another parachute demonstration. If they did drop supplies they were for some other camp, for we were doomed to disappointment. Only one small bundle was seen dropped but I don't know if it was worth picking up.

Received details of fatigue party for tomorrow, of which I am to take charge. While detailing other members of the party the lights came on in the huts. Most unexpected and most acceptable.

Today two men painted the word 'THANKS' on the roof of the new building so the planes would see we appreciated their efforts.

A news bulletin was put upon the notice-board. It had been extracted from newspapers received with the recently dropped supplies. Details of the atomic bomb and its destructive power were given. We came to the conclusion the curious cloud of smoke in the sky seen by some of the lads was none other than Hiroshima going up in smoke about seventy miles away. I did not see this myself, but if it is true it just shows what a terribly infernal thing the bomb is. No wonder these people packed in. They had no alternative!

August 31st

I had put my name down to go for an early morning run and swim. Thought I would risk this strenuous exercise as an experiment as I feel a bit fitter since getting some better food, but as it was pouring with rain the whole thing was called off.

Started my fatigue party working. Rather a complicated matter as two men were reporting sick, and I was left in the air about replacements. Had just sorted it out when the planes came over and started dropping; more supplies.

We had a really exciting time. Some of the chutes actually came down in the camp. On two occasions I decided the swaying oil drums were coming too close and dived down an air raid shelter, discretion being the better part of valour.

About a dozen loads were dropped, up to twelve parachutes coming down each time. I doubt you can picture what a lovely sight it was to see the various coloured chutes descending – reds, whites, blues, yellows, greens; and all for us. In fact, so much stuff was dropped the letters 'PW' formed on the parade ground with white roofing tiles were hurriedly changed to the word 'STOP'. Even so, one or two loads were dropped after this.

Orders were given for everybody to fall in to go out to collect the swag. Even I was sent out, in spite of protesting I was on work of primary importance. Of course, I preferred salvage work to supervising emptying latrines so I did not press the point.

Found myself left to mind a double canister that had broken away from its chute and come down a very heavy bump. The canister consisted of two oil drums ('Gasoline' was still clearly marked on them) welded together. Amused myself by salvaging as much as I could from the lake of tomato soup and fruit juice inside the drum. Of course, I licked my fingers pretty often, especially when handling a tin of chicken, beans and rice, mixed fruit, or other rather attractive contents. Permission was given for us to eat what we wished on the job, so I'm confessing to no crime. I suppose I ate more than thought, for I found tiffin rather a problem. There was the thickest stew I've had in this camp, and bags of it; fruit drink, dumplings and duff. I ate more than I should and felt very uncomfortable all the afternoon. I could eat very little for tea.

In the afternoon I was told to collect my fatigue party and get on with emptying the benjo. By more good luck than judgement I found a couple of men and set them to work for half an hour. After that the job had 'had it', for the others were out collecting; and I in my turn got collected for the job of shifting wet kit to a fresh store. By this time it was raining hard and I had the privilege of getting soaked. That did have the advantage of making me appreciate a hot bath when I had finished.

September 1st

Place on wash bench being pinched by someone, so I was forced to sleep inside. In spite of a liberal sprinkling of insecticide the bugs enjoyed a good feast, although many paid dearly for their gluttony.

A very busy day for me as I was both mess orderly and billet orderly. I had my hands so full I had to take half my bread cob on parade with me while I still had a mouthful. Net result, a ticking off by 'Bunny'.

Spent all day collecting parachuted supplies. When we knocked off there were still some left, over which a piquet was mounted. Much to our disgust a plane came over and dropped another load near the camp. We don't want it: we have more than enough already. In fact we are heartily glad some men came from another camp that had been sadly neglected as regards clothing and cigarettes.

Where I was working today the Yank was hanging around. He told us that on the first air drop three people were killed (so it was true after all). Four more were supposed to have been killed by the second air drop. There have been numerous casualties among the civilians and Petrovsky (our MO) was called out to perform several amputations. It seems such a shame this should happen as a result of this operation of mercy, and now that the war is over.

Note: the Yank was a Jap who had lived in America most of his life. Evidently he had been in Japan when the war started and had been prevented from returning to the USA.

He spoke broad American and could not read a Japanese newspaper. He had to get the 'Nippon Times', printed in English. When he had read it he gave it to one of us.

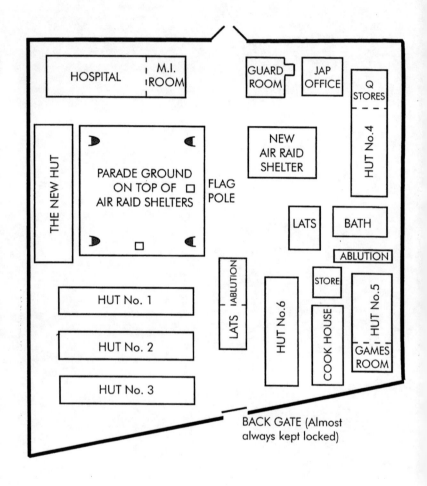

Plan of POW camp at Ube

September 2nd, Sunday

Another day collecting supplies. Allocated to collecting parachutes. Our party made the job easier by commandeering a couple of handcarts, one of which we gave to another less enterprising party. Two journeys would have seen the job done, but while we were loading the cart for the second time some B29s (everybody says they are B29s) which had been circling around for a while started dropping more supplies! How strange it must have been to see us gazing up at an approaching plane and, when we saw the bomb bays open, fervently praying, 'For goodness' sake don't drop anything!' When they did, you should have heard the exclamations of disgust!

On our way back to camp with our second load of chutes we decided to follow the example of other parties, take the law into our own hands, dump the chutes by the wayside and make for the stuff we could eat. Our career was a short one, however, for we met Mr Fitt. He collared all available men to construct a sign on a piece of waste ground saying 'DROP HERE' if they must ignore our 'STOP' sign, so as to avoid the risk of damaging more houses and killing more people.

I was left in charge of my handcart. I made my way to 'the square' of the town – the local parade ground or something, with a shrine in the corner. A load had landed there and I was soon loading up with the help of some Japs, and was on my way back to camp before reinforcements arrived.

An announcement was made that those who wanted dental treatment were to parade at the MI room. Hearing the dentist was really 'hot stuff' I decided to go. He was good! He whipped out a back one in next to no time and as cleanly as a whistle using a very good local anaesthetic called 'Tercain', I think it was called, which acted quicker than anything I've had previously. While over at the MI room I stepped on the scales turning them at 60.4 kilos plus hat, shorts, boots and tooth about to come out. They can be counted as about three kilos. That means nearly seven kilos gained since August 11th. I shall soon be back to normal at this rate.

Volunteered to turn tailor and help make a Union Jack out of coloured parachute materials. This kept me occupied until tea time. Some lad brought in the medical orderly's autograph book after tea. Seeing others signed I thought I'd do the same.

September 3rd

Reported for flag making but found enthusiasm slack – only one other turned up apart from the sergeant-major who was responsible for the business. Stuck it for most of the morning but began to feel a mug, so packed it in when tiffin came. Conveniently 'forgot' to go back in the afternoon and heard no more about it. Perhaps the whole project has been scrapped and some attempt will be made to obtain one from a boat in the harbour. Anyway, the one we are making will blow to pieces within five minutes of being put up the flagpole.

This evening Ted Howard died. How very hard to have come right through to the very day peace was being signed and then die when one could visualise being home very soon.

September 4th

Another rainy day. I spent most of the time making a backpack out of canvas from one of the bales that came down by parachute. Collected a parachute from which I hope to get a panel as a souvenir.

This afternoon the funeral of Ted Howard took place. We were brought to attention by the 'fall in' on the trumpet. A short service was held in the dining hall and the 'Last Post' was sounded. For some reason I do not know the 'Reveille' did not follow. The coffin was then brought out and taken away on a lorry covered with the flag I had helped to make. I'm glad I helped with it now as it made possible that touch which seems so essentially a part of a soldier's funeral. The flag under which he served and under which he is still found even when death has robbed him of his power to serve. If we wish to be sentimental we can remark that the country he served, in its turn, now serves him and recognises the debt it owes him.

I scalded my leg yesterday boiling water at the steam pipe. It's worse than I thought it was and has come up in a big water blister. I must go sick with it in the morning.

Different messing arrangements today so as to give the cooks a rest. Some think they don't deserve it, but I should like to remember these cooks as the fairest and even the most industrious I have met in the army. I do not begrudge them a day off.

September 5th

Went sick this morning. After painful treatment I learnt I was 'C' for the day. Used the opportunity to do some washing. Strange to be able to use soap extravagantly. Then helped myself to several pieces of parachute, all of different colours (they were being left to rot in a pile on the square) and planned all sorts of things to make from them.

September 6th

Evidence that we were now the boss. After breakfast a squad of men were imported to do fatigues such as emptying the benjo, clearing up the rubbish, cleaning the ablutions, etc. Whether they were Koreans as many said, or pure blooded Nips, I don't know.

Sick parade again this morning with the added complication of a swollen foot and ankle. It looks suspiciously like wet beri-beri; anyway, the MO ordered me to keep off my hind legs as much as possible. Settled down to making that much-needed pack I had cut out two days ago from a piece of canvas.

September 7th

Not required to see the MO this morning, but still under orders to rest my legs; so I was able to finish making my pack, although I might add some pockets. Borrowed a piece of indelible pencil from J. E. in return for putting his name on his kit bag. Treated my newly-made pack in the same way.

Traded some of my fags, giving two cartons of two hundred for a box of fifty bars of chocolate. Even after three and a half years I have not forgotten how to enjoy chocolate. In a more furtive manner (through the fence) got seven or eight onions for twenty cigarettes; and five tomatoes for the same number.

We were disgusted to have another parachute drop. The novelty has worn off and we are sure we will never need the stuff. Brightened up when we found we were not required to bring the supplies into the camp; this task being given to our squad of Nip cleaners, under supervision. They get two yen a day from the mining company, and a midday meal, a packet of fags and a bar of chocolate from us as payment. This is by far the better idea. We are rapidly degenerating to the condition of the average British soldier abroad.

Filled my newly-made pack with most of my clean gear. Words of praise from others made me feel my pride was justified.

September 8th

Two more days 'C' given me, as although the scald is getting better my legs are still swollen. Rather annoying as it prevents me going out. Small groups are allowed into the locality, while excursions further afield have been organised. Visits have been made to other POW camps about twenty miles away.

Made a small kit bag and tacked up the bottom of my new slacks which are too long for me.

Medical note – Feet swollen up worse than ever. Must cut out liquids and sweet stuff, which I have not been able to do up till now.

September 9th

I had to keep off my legs as much as possible so just pottered around doing very little. We had another issue of odds and ends: chocolate, cigarettes, matches and (as the highlight of the whole 'presento') a complete box of twenty packets of chewing gum!

Very disgusted no arrangements were made for a service today, except for the RCs who went down into Ube to the local church where a German priest was. A nice man by all accounts, but leaving the district tomorrow. On the whole a quiet day.

September 10th

Had the novel experience of being photographed today. 'Les' wanted a snap of part of the camp and thought it would be improved with a few figures in the foreground. He had just bought this camera and some plates for it. I hope it comes out. I should like to have one.

While at sick parade this morning and waiting for a dressing on my foot, I stepped on the scales. The needle swung to sixty-five kilos – an increase of about fifteen kilos in the last month.

Still have not found out why there was no church service last night. Several of the lads discussed the omission in my hearing and agreed it was a disgrace. One quoted Kipling with the words 'Lest we forget'. I find such an attitude encouraging for it shows there are still many who are not indifferent to the fact there is a God above who deserves thanks and praise not only for victory, but for personal preservation.

September 11th

The MO judged my leg was doing so well I could come off 'C' and do 'light duties'. Must see him again in three days.

A party returned from another camp where they had hoped to collect some mail and told us fifty or sixty men were grabbed at ten minutes' notice to go by plane on the first hop of their evacuation. They went with only what they stood in. It gave me complex food for thought as I have so many things I want to keep.

September 15th

The last four days have been crammed so full of excitement and bustle I have not found time to record what happened. Or, as Jane Austen nearly said, 'I have failed during the last four days to make any entries in my journal, being somewhat overcome by the pressure of recent events.'

Wednesday (12th) put us in a ferment of excitement when Orders went up announcing we had to be packed and ready to move on the morrow. Scuttled round to finish my kitbag and pack as much as I could.

My cargo capacity looked like being severely overtaxed, so to cut down on my kit I investigated 'the Market'. If you pick up a 'thriller' filled with crooks and underworld you read of 'the fence', through whom you dispose of the 'jools'. In our case the fence was real and wooden. It separated us from the ultimate holders of the traded articles so we picked holes in it. Holes appeared in that fence as profusely and mysteriously as bug bites do when you are in bed. Round every hole business was in progress and trade was brisk.

I sold some cigarettes and sprung from poverty to possible prosperity in five minutes, getting 450 yen. My greatcoat failed to sell, so I left it behind where, no doubt, it was discovered by some grateful guy. Well, it was disgracefully shabby and fit only for a Japanese back or the dustbin.

Later in the morning 'PW supplies' came over and although I went down to the beach in case, they did not drop anything.

Orderly sergeant came round and said all walking out leave was being stopped after tonight, so we had best make the best of the afternoon.

This announcement spurred me on to hurry into town although improperly dressed in singlet instead of shirt and in spite of swollen legs. Philosophy employed – 'My legs can't be too bad if I can get my boots on.'

My main objective was the Post Office, although my motive was not purely philatelic. My eye was more to business. I reasoned if the Yen fell to such a level that its value might be a minus quantity I would be better off if I turned my yen into stamps. The weight was the same and the market guaranteed a fair price if one took the trouble to look for it.

But what is the good of theory without efficient practical application? The PO (notice the absence of the horribly familiar 'W') found I got down to business. The girl behind the counter had no sense. Either that, or my Japanese just isn't. I never was much good at languages, and I freely admit what Japanese I know could be put on the back of a postage stamp; but I refuse to countenance the suggestion that when I speak Nipponese the result is worse than useless.

Business consisted of asking for stamps – an easy enough thing to do by dumb show, sign language, rule of thumb, or whatever other name you call that universal way of communication. A convenient envelope helped me to do the trick, but when it came to quantity and quality 'taxan' (meaning 'big', 'lots', 'plenty', etc.) was definitely wide of the mark. 'All' applied as pidgin English was no better; and a recitation of the values taken haphazardly from one sen to one yen was greeted with a shake of the head and little better success. 'Perseverance' may not be my middle name either literally or metaphorically, but I'll claim I showed a little of that on this occasion. It was like squeezing blood out of a stone to get her to produce stamps from a little cabinet at her elbow. The episode ended with me walking out of the PO with eight varieties of stamps in blocks of ten. I had spent Y12.70 all told. Little did that girl know I was prepared to spend Y212.70 on stamps. Annoyed with myself at not doing better I resolved to make amends on the morrow if possible.

'Possible' it wasn't; or if it was, it was most inconvenient. I didn't find time to redeem my shortcomings. What made matters worse was that on comparing notes with a brother philatelist (if I may presume to call myself that), I found he had about twice as many varieties as myself; but (stupid man) as he had only bought one specimen of each I knew it would be useless to ask him to sell me any. Mine was a clear case of Miss Fortune only knocking once on my door. That might not sound right, but it looks okay on paper.

I must not forget to mention the journey back to camp, which was almost epic in its way. I had linked up with a couple of lads also out for a stroll. One of them hailed a passing car. We piled in, in spite of Orders that 'Vehicles *must not* be commandeered for private use: the practice will cease forthwith, etc., etc.' When within a stone's throw of the camp we stopped and hopped out – a sure sign of a guilty conscience. Before abandoning ship (or car) completely I pulled out of my pocket a packet of chewing gum and handed it over with that 'keep the change' air. In return I received an obsequious nod of the napper.

That night I slept on the wash bench for the last time, although I did not know that at the time. All we knew was we were to be packed and ready for 'take off'. We were allowed one heavy bag, and one light container to travel with us. My pack held twice as much as my newly-made kit bag but that did not stop me handing in as 'heavy' the one that was far lighter. In spite of orders I also had a side haversack and a water bottle (which had been left behind by a roommate).

The order to move (on Thursday) caused tremendous confusion when it came. We were just sitting down to our midday meal when told we were to move in half an hour. I say 'we', meaning the other nine chaps in the room. I was still under the doctor and felt covered by the term 'any sort of sick'. That meant I was not affected by the order.

Scatter here, scatter there; hurry, rush and tear: and as when the whirlwind passes all becomes quiet, so I am left alone in the room amidst the debris of a hurried departure. The midday meal had been ignored, but fortunately, being mostly in tins and boxes, distribution could be made. I was left with a tin of peas to carry.

As the anaesthetic of the sudden stillness wore off I took literal stock of my surroundings. First I ate. There was plenty of food around and I ate unwisely. I felt decidedly convex instead of concave, but can't say I was feeling a better shape. Then I got down to business.

There were masses of stuff left behind including soap, chewing gum and cigarettes. The market, however, was bearing out the economic laws of supply and demand. A mental sign had been apparently hoisted declaring: 'These goods must be cleared at any price.' Further influence on prices was caused by so many lads giving stuff away. It seems strange that some of the most generous were the very men who two months ago were boasting in no uncertain manner of what they would do to the Nips if they had but half the chance to lay their hands on them. Scarcely could they open their mouths without slandering the Nips' origins; while the thought of showing goodwill, let alone giving them anything was furthest from their minds.

I'm no psychologist so had better confine myself to my own experiences. I've no personal love for these people – at least, not sufficient at the moment to make me philanthropic towards them. I wanted what I could get for my supplies. I entered the market full of hope and with a pleasantly plentiful supply of goods. I was in for a shock.

Wherever I approached the fence hands would shoot through the nearest holes and children's voices would chant 'Chewing gum-o' or 'Cigarett-o'. I refused to be drawn. Prices had fallen dramatically, nevertheless when I ceased trading for the day I had netted Y230.

At about 5.30 p.m. we left the camp. Buses had been dug up from somewhere and we travelled to the station in style; no overcrowding being the order of the day. These buses had been converted to gas-driven vehicles, the gas being generated in a coke stove behind. By the way they wound them up, you would have thought they were being driven by clockwork.

Eventually our engine came to life and away we went up the unmade, pot-holey road to the concrete road leading past the gas and chemical works to the station. I was looking at Ube for the last time.

There is no need for me to describe that journey to our port of embarkation. It was the most comfortable journey I have had since I left England. Put it down as similar to travelling in saloon coaches in war-torn England on a train that was 'full' but not overcrowded. Just a few spare seats, and we went at a reasonable speed. I understand the Japanese are very proud of their railways and I'll say this much for them, they are the best thing I have encountered in Japan.

Japan is beautiful – that is an accident and not the fault of the Nips so we need not hesitate to say so. Much of our journey lay along the coast, and frequently I was reminded of south Devon by the rocky bays and headlands we passed. All that was missing were the deep red cliffs. In other places there were pleasantly chaotic mountain formations – not extensive but compact.

We had plenty of food with us. At the end of our journey I regretfully had to throw some of it away. I still could not appreciate that I was soon to be back in the world of plenty.

We arrived at Wakayama at about 4 a.m. on Friday. This was the end of our train journey. We hardly had time to stop before we were greeted by the sound of a band playing unmistakably Western tunes. They swung into tunes that will never die, like 'Pack Up Your Troubles': songs that bridge four years, and leave you with tonsillitis or some similar complaint. Three and a half years as a POW made me very sentimental, and it is amazing how such a little thing can raise a lump in one's throat.

As we listened to the band we could see nurses passing down the platform to another coach where the stretcher cases were. I don't think it was so much the sight of white women that raised an additional lump as the knowledge we had come down so close to home as to be in the same world as they. A world that spoke of civilisation and promised peace.

The band stopped playing and a pleasant face under a peaked cap looked in the window with an 'Anybody want an *English* cigarette?' Only an Englishman could have put over such a sentence with such expression. How else could he know that however good a Camel or a Chesterfield might be, an Englishman prefers his Players and his Capstan. As a non-smoker I was impressed by the expressions of delight from those around me at having a

Capstan between their lips or a Players in their hand to be puffed at.

Then came our turn to de-train: our time to be transported.

Dawn broke on Friday and scattered the light of early day upon a scene of devastation and ruin: the mute witness to severe air raids. We were taken by tram past it all. As we rattled along they gave us a bar of chocolate and a stencilled newspaper. From the tram we went for a cursory inspection at which medical officers asked us if we felt more or less fit, and what were our complaints? We were lined up in two ranks and one MO came down each rank. If he was not satisfied he yanked you out to go as a stretcher case. I succeeded in avoiding capture and went to a waiting landing barge – one of those craft which had featured so prominently during this war, and which were to impress me before long with their general utility.

From barge to beach we proceeded from beach to hotel where delousing, medical inspection, breakfast and cablegrams were attended to.

Before we entered the hotel we had been told to dump our kit as we could only take one package of personal belongings. I followed the example of those ahead and made my package a large one containing as much as possible. Why throw away brand new gear?

The hotel strongly resembled a disturbed anthill. From here you went there, from doing this you went and did that. You finished talking to this man and turned to another. Looking back on it puts one's memory in a turmoil.

First we were given a number which was painted on our chests in iodine while we were told not to forget it. Mine was 1920. Then we washed it off in the showers with genuine Lifebuoy soap. From the bath we made our way to an encounter with the latest secret weapon in the form of a sort of 'Flit' spray that peppered us with insecticide, via a renumbering ceremony (more iodine) to the clothing department. Vest, pants, slacks, shirt and socks rigged us out in a pleasant light and dark blue colour scheme.

Then to the doctors – crowds of them. They wrote things down knowing just which part of the form to fill in: which was just as well because I didn't. I fed, having my first introduction to American bread, which is very good. Very, very light so you think you are eating a lot. After that I sent my cablegram home.

Another room was labelled something about 'War Criminals'. To my relief it wasn't me in trouble this time. I was required to fill in a form giving details of atrocities I knew about or had witnessed. As you might expect, I could not remember any details now I wanted them. Incidents I could recollect were insufficient in detail to be of any use. I wrote something noncommittal.

On the form was another question: 'Had I kept a diary of some sort?' I put down 'Yes' although I doubted it would be any good to them if they asked for it.

In another room we had to fill in forms about ourselves under the careful direction of 2nd Lieutenant Cain – whoever he was. His name had to go down on one of the many dotted lines. There was something frightful printed at the bottom of one side about penalties for giving false information. Something calculated to make one's memory function accurately about promotions.

I was through! Outside the hotel I claimed my 'personal kit package' – my large home-made pack.

Down on the beach again, to my surprise, I found my 'heavy' kit. I thought I had seen the last of that.

Then aboard a waiting LSD and over the waves to the *Consolation*. A hospital ship has a surprising look about it. Its purity of intention is so obvious from its pure whiteness. Its red crosses and green line speak of honesty of purpose – telling the world to witness it has no quarrel that requires her to put on a dingy grey coat to sneak about the oceans seeking either to destroy or to avoid destruction.

Up the gangway – a question or two from another doctor: the assignment to a ward – and the first stage of our repatriation is really over. We are free! We are among friends! We are *going home*!

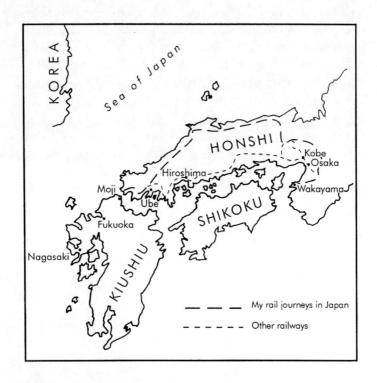

Southern Japan

From Moji I was taken to Ube by train to work down the coal mine (via a tunnel under the sea). Hiroshima was about seventy miles away. Upon release we were taken by train to Wakayama. Note the long way round to avoid the devastation, but we did see the outskirts of Osaka.

Stories Told by Prisoners of War

In the prison camps, after a tiring and often traumatic day's work, we were in no condition for either energetic occupation or intellectual effort. Mostly our only light was a flickering wick in a bath of coconut oil. For much of the time we were forbidden pencils and paper: those were the days when the very notes from which these stories are remembered were tucked in the waistband of my shorts. There was only one thing to do – sit around and talk. We sat in pairs or groups and talked; our conversations fell naturally into the channel of swapping yarns about our experiences. Unlike most barrack room stories, which seemed to deal mostly with wine and women, ours turned to food, as though we sought to fill our stomachs with words when our meagre rations failed. That was a subject I could enter upon. Often, when down the mine, and after eating my 'binto' (or 'snap' as our English miners would say) we would chat about nothing else.

The stories I shall tell here are of two types. First, the experiences we swapped as POWs, then I shall recall other stories of army life from earlier days: they are good ones and raised a laugh when we heard them. Some even have a moral which sets them aside from the frivolous accounts of debauchery far too many take a pride in recounting.

Roberts Hospital

Quizzes, of various types, were among our most popular forms of entertainment, and I often took part. Usually daylight had gone and lighting was inadequate, giving ample opportunity for unseen prompting by fellow members of your team – which, I'm afraid, we did.

The quiz master whistled a tune and asked me to verify it, which I couldn't. My team mate whispered a three syllable word of which I only heard the last, 'sweet'. Brightly I answered 'Meadowsweet'.

'That's right,' said the QM. 'Bittersweet'; and we got the point.

In a POW Working Party Camp in Singapore (River Valley or Havelock Road)

The black market is rampant and the lads are buying tins of bully beef etc. from the natives through the fence. When the supply of tins is exhausted the natives tell the prisoners to dig in the floor of their hut. They do, and unearth cases of tins buried by the natives before the huts were taken over for a POW camp.

In River Valley Camp

Perhaps I should explain our faces were our strongest chains as POWs. We could not hide them, or disguise them as Asiatic; so that wherever we went we were immediately recognised. This is why we could be let out of camp without supervision.

Three lads scrounged a barrow and shovel and boldly walked out of the camp 'nodding' to the sentry as they went. Obviously they were bound for some sand required for some job in the camp – a perfectly legitimate fatigue. They went to a big pile of sand behind a row of Chinese huts. There they started to fill the barrow. One shovelful, then an expectant look round. They had not long to wait before the Chinese offered them coffee and biscuits, eggs and bacon. Having eaten and put another shovelful of sand in the barrow they proceeded to the next pile of sand where the same ploy was adopted. Two hours later the three are entering the camp with half a barrow of sand and full tummies. A dutiful 'nod' to the sentry as they pass and all is well.

As you may easily guess, this racket was worked too much. At last the Nips realised the fatigue was self-imposed and took steps to stop it.

In Havelock Road

So securely did our faces hold us it was not uncommon for the Japanese sentry to give his rifle to a prisoner to mind. One story tells how one lad took a Nip rifle to pieces and took out the ammunition. My notes are not very clear but I think this was done in front of the Nip and at his request.

While on this subject; on the journey up to Siam a Nip soldier gave his rifle to a British sergeant-major to mind!

Bangpong (End of the Rail Journey to Siam)

A small party was detailed to take some heavy pieces of wood and follow a Nip. They stop and the Nip disappears. Another Nip appears and leads them another two hundred yards and stops outside a hut. A third Nip appears and indicates the wood is to be moved elsewhere. In lurid language one justly exasperated member of the party explodes, 'I wish these blankety blank blue-pencil so-and-sos would make up their minds!'

'Say you guys!' Everyone looked round to see who had spoken but all they saw was another Nip who had come out of another hut. They gaped as he started speaking with a broad American accent. 'You'd better be careful what you say round here, some of these guys understand English. You're browned off, are you? What about me? I have to eat and sleep with the bastards!'

He had lived nearly all his life in America and was visiting Japan for a holiday just before the war broke out. He wanted to go back there. I wonder what the people there will think.

Bangbong – British Officers' Mess

Told to me by Ginger with whom I became great pals. When working in the mess he was caught by a Nip sentry giving rice to a Thai child. The Nip bashed the poor kid and also hit Ginger. Off they went to the officers, but they could not help poor Ginger who was obviously in for trouble. The Nip led Ginger to believe that he was going to be bayoneted. The Nip marched him over to the QM, whom Ginger was well in with. He tried to tip the QM the wink to say the rice was no good but the Nip understood and gave him another blow for his pains. Then he was led to the guardroom where the story was explained to the guard commander. Fortunately he saw the funny side and laughed. The interpreter explained that giving away rice caused ill-feeling and was therefore forbidden. Ginger went away very relieved.

Bangpong During the Floods

In this camp we slept on bamboo platforms raised about three feet above the ground. When the person who told this story went to bed to get a little sleep before going on duty the hut was dry. The man he was to relieve came to wake him up with a casual 'Careful how you get out, there's two feet of water here.'

On this occasion the latrine trenches overflowed and the cookhouse was drowned so no fires could be lit. When a hut collapsed, and its evacuation was organised, the cry went up 'Women and children first!' You can always trust someone to make a joke no matter what the circumstances.

It was about this time that the 'Loyals' found a snake under their hut, no doubt driven there by the rising water. As it was night and the snake seemed intent on sleeping they left it and settled down. One lad, wishing to speak to his sleeping neighbour, pinched him, with the result that he jumped clean out of his mosquito net as though he had been bitten.

I think it was in Bangpong or Kanjong-buri that one of our MOs (Major Pemberton I believe) amputated a limb. For want of surgical instruments he had to use an ordinary saw.

While talking of operations, I remember hearing that when seventeen thousand of us were concentrated in the five hundred by three hundred yards of the Selarang Barracks a doctor operated on a man for acute appendicitis.

Chungkai

One lad pointed to wound scars on his friend's back and told a Nip 'Singapore bang! bang!' The Nip, not willing to be outdone, searched his own limbs for scars and finding some, pointed them out as Singapore wounds. To our knowledge these Nips were never there, although they reeled off noted battles such as Sergarmat, Allastaire and Ipoh. The scars were from tropical ulcers.

I always associate Taramoto with Chungkai for that is where I met him and saw the callous way he ordered the man I was working with to carry on after nearly cutting off his fingers while emptying a little truck. If ever I wanted to hit a man, I did then. It would have been suicide to have done so.

This same man hated the British. When he saw some lads puzzling over the meaning of a notice pinned on the board he said it meant 'You must work harder'. He could speak good English but never would except as a last resort. He is supposed to have said he was going to return to Edinburgh after the war to finish his education. The 'Jocks' have expressed their intention of looking out for him if he does. No one liked Taramoto.

Kinsio – A Camp I Spent One Night in when Passing Up-country

A Nip caught a man slacking and made him stand in the sun holding a shovel above his head. In half an hour 'yasmi' time came and the party was allowed to rest while this man had to keep standing. When he lowered the shovel a little the Nip bashed him and made him raise it again. When he lowered it again the Nip seized a bamboo stick and gave him six slashes, knocking him senseless to the ground, and then walked away. Another Nip came along and was human enough to sprinkle some water on him. When the medical orderly came he had to attend to a slight cut on the Nip's hand before he could touch the man on the ground.

Another story from Kinsio, where meat was very scarce. The lads actually ate crocodile, monkey and dog; so I am told. When they were given a dead chimpanzee (?) it looked so human they could not touch it so they threw it in the river. One night a Japanese sentry was seen suddenly to charge across the parade ground and bayonet a dog – no doubt for practice. He offered it to our cooks but they refused it. But whether someone did take it I cannot say because one day there was 'leggy' meat stew, which was excellent and rather like ox-tail soup. The men queued up for more, but its nice taste turned to bitterness when the cooks asked 'Did you like the dog stew?'

I understand crocodile tastes very oily.

Eating queer things reminds me of when working on the garden in the countryside outside Ube. Someone caught a snake and we cooked it over a little fire. We all sampled it. I cannot give an opinion on the taste except to say it was not unpleasant, and nor did it make us ill.

Kenyu – An Area I Only Passed Through

In one of the Kenyu camps there was so much sickness the work was falling far behind schedule. If you could stand up you were fit enough for work, and in vain our doctors put men in hospital. The Nips came round and if you were not nearly dead, out you went to work. I heard that men were carried out on stretchers and placed beside the track to break up stones for ballast.

Tonchien Camps – Above Tarsoh

In one of this group of camps we lost 120 men in two weeks due to the cholera. The Tamils working on the railway nearby lost four times this number. Big pits were dug and the Tamils were laid on the edge. The Nip guard ordered them to be tipped into the pit as soon as he was satisfied they were dead. Forty to fifty a day died at this time. One Tamil, upon being tipped into the pit, sat up; but the Nip had said he was dead so seizing a shovel he bashed him on the head. He *was* dead then. Some of them wandered off into the woods to die. A Nip coming upon a prostrate figure sent for a stretcher. When it came the man woke up from his after-tiffin nap and, seeing the stretcher, let out a yell and dashed into the woods, never to be seen again. I'm sure many natives died of fright rather than the cholera.

Cholera was deadly. I heard of one man who at tiffin time was in the 'leggy' queue. Before the next meal he had died – of cholera!

Perhaps there was some justification for the Nip guard who, in charge of a party going down country to a hospital camp, took into the jungle and shot a man who had developed cholera en route.

This brings me to a note that tells me it was estimated that up to May 1943 twelve thousand had died while working on the railway. The note goes on: 'The Nips are supposed to say they estimate one third would die before it is finished. It must be finished at all costs!'

Another note gives the cost of drugs at Tamakan. I'm not sure of the currency but I think it is Thai 'dollars'. Certain injections cost up to twenty-five a time. Roller bandages cost two dollars and squares of lint ten. Tablets cost a half each. A thousand dollars go nowhere.

While on the subject of sickness I turn to my 'One Line Diary for 1945': March 27. 'First solid 'stool' for months (seven actually). Good! (up to this time have been subject to the 'squitters since in Japan.' It didn't last. Had a relapse after a couple of days.

Brencassi Camp

American aircraft flying overhead. A Nip tried to pull down the Japanese flag, but it jammed, so he seized an axe and cut down the flagpole. Some of our camps in Siam were actually bombed.

Ten Kilometres Short of Takanun

We had to change trains here because the steam trains went no farther at this time. Only diesel lorries with adapted wheels were used on the next section. The empty trucks ahead were shunted off and the lorry was connected up in front. It started off with only one truck. 'Wo back!' Back it came and connected up again. This time it went off with only three trucks. Third time was lucky and away we went, helped on our way by three men with flags, the driver, a spare man and Taramoto, who had moved up to this camp from Chungkai. I've often wondered what he thought of this performance.

Takanun

One of the men in our tent got a craze for giving strange nicknames to the others. None of your 'Chalky White' or 'Dusty Miller'. One lad named Pearson he started calling 'Armour'. I asked him why. He logically replied, 'Well, "armour piercin".' I did not escape from his inventiveness for he called me 'Takka', which was just as logical because the name of the camp we were in was Takanun.

I must just slip in here the tale of the Dutch padre who underwent an operation. They started before he was properly 'out', whereupon he sat up and cried, 'Oh! you've started too soon!' I don't think it was the same padre I met at Tamakan, whom I hold in great affection.

The Japanese Guardroom – A Typical Form of Punishment

When put in the guardroom for five days this lad found the guard used any excuse to give him a bashing. When he called to the sentry (to ask permission to go to 'benjo') he called out 'Nippon!' Bash! 'Not Nippon, must say "Japan".' The next time, when he called 'Japan!' he got another bash: 'Not Japan, must say "Nippon".' When asked by the guard 'Churchill No. 1?' he said, 'Yes.' Bash! Then he said 'No.' Bash! Then he tried 'Tojo No. 1.' Bash! Nothing was right.

He had to sweep out the guardroom, first sprinkling a little water. Bash! 'Not enough water.' The Nip seized the bucket and emptied it over the floor. Bash! Too much water now. He had to take some exercise so he was told to run round the guardhouse. As he disappeared round the back the guard calls 'Hey! You escape!' Bash! He had to sit up all day: if he leant back; 'Hey! You go to sleep!' Bash!

The Japanese Character

From Java comes the story of three men who tried to escape. They were caught and bayoneted in front of the whole camp before anything could be done.

Shortly after capitulation in Singapore a Nip soldier is said to have cut off a girl's hand because she gave food to a prisoner.

When a prisoner struck a Nip who spat in his face he was put in the guardroom for seven days trussed up with a rope and frequently beaten. He was so badly treated that when he came out he permanently bore the scars of the ropes. He was kept alive with chicken broth smuggled in to him as tea.

I have mentioned Selarang already. I was told that connected with that affair was the shooting of four men at Changi. They were Captain Phillips, a sergeant, a Eurasian and one other who were part of a legitimate ration party outside the camp. My notes suggest they were shot to induce a riot because we had refused to sign the papers promising not to escape. Perhaps it is no wonder we sometimes think the Nips were inhuman. I know much of what they did was in order to get tangible results – it was important for them to save face; but that does not justify much of what they did.

One guard went to the English cookhouse for some meat for his dog. The cooks refused. At about midnight he walked into the cookhouse with a kitten on his bayonet and roasted it over one of the fires.

They could be generous too, in a strange sort of way. One man, out of bed in the middle of the night to go to the benjo met a guard on patrol with an English sergeant-major. 'Johnny,' asked the Nip, 'you English?' 'Yes.' 'You sleep all night?' 'Yes.' 'Him sergeant-major no sleep all night. You bow to Nippon soldier but say nothing to him! You bow and say "Thank you very much Sergeant-Major".' The most tactful thing to do was to obey, so he did.

The pettiness if their character comes out in this incident in a barber's shop. Barbers have a habit of wiping soapy razors on a piece of old newspaper. While Jock was shaving a Nip guard his mate was performing on another customer and wiping his razor on a piece of newspaper which happened to have a photograph of the Emperor's son and heir. On the reverse was a picture of Tojo. The Nip considered this an insult to the leaders of his country, so he lined up everyone in the shop and, after an explanation, bashed them all. Jock, being the one shaving the Nip, got off with a token tap (even Nips have respect for a razor). The last one in the line was the client with a lathered face. The Nip wipes the lather off and onto the lad's shorts. Bash! He wipes his hand again, pockets the offending paper and goes off.

In one of the camps a Nip guard fancied himself at judo and liked to practise his throws on convenient and unbelligerent prisoners. One lad got fed up with being thrown about. He stood up and said to the guard, 'Dummy, dummy! (No good!) In England we do this,' and landed a beautiful upper-cut. The Nip got up, bowed as though at the end of a friendly contest he was acknowledging defeat, and went off.

A Nip sentry came into a hut and saw a chess set. Taking off his boots and leaning his rifle somewhere he played one of our lads. The game finished, he patted the prisoner on the shoulder and said, 'England number one, Germany finished,' and putting on his boots, went off.

All these stories were told when we had time to sit around and talk. They are hearsay and I cannot vouch for their accuracy. But I do remember one Nip coming into the office (I can't remember what I was doing there), and sitting down, completely browned off. Laboriously he asked how long we thought the war would last. We had heard some very heartening rumours lately so before anybody could give the game away I said, 'Two years.'

'Two years?' he responded, in an anguished voice. 'No, two months!' We hoped so too. 'No like guards,' he confided; and then asked, 'Why must there be war?' Apparently he had spent a year in China and more than a year here in Siam. Not all Nips were that bad.

I remember during a break in our work filling cement bags ready for use down the mine on construction work sitting in a hut out of the bitterly cold wind, when a Nip came in and sat down. He pulled out a packet of cigarettes, saw there were ten of us there, broke some in half and gave them to us. I did not want to slight his friendly act, so although a non-smoker I took my half, pretended to puff at it, and then slipped it to my grateful neighbour.

A Hero for Ten Minutes

I had the doubtful privilege of getting forty miles up the mainland of Malaya before the Japs got there. My troop commander sent me back to HQ for rations, telling me to pop right back into Johore Bahru and try to get some beer for the lads. Time was short as I had to get there before the shops were shut so I stepped on the gas. Johore was all closed up, but I found two lads who knew where beer was to be found if we could get across the Causeway. We got across and got the beer – seventy-two bottles of it, carefully tucked in the back. We even managed to get some petrol to make sure we had enough to get us back to camp. We picked up our rations and started back. Several times I heard a shrill whistle and thought my engine had developed a fault, but when I stopped I found it was only the crickets whistling; and whistling so loud that it made my ears feel funny. A waving torch brought us to a halt, only to be told to proceed without lights. We did, and nearly knocked an oncoming car off the road in the darkness. We were hopelessly late by now and arrived at camp to find anxious faces. They had heard the road was cut by the Japs and thought that was the last they would see of the beer. For ten minutes at least, I'm sure I was a hero in their eyes. I hope so because I don't drink.

Singapore

During the battle for Singapore I was standing in the shack that was troop headquarters when we heard the familiar sound that followed the appearance of twenty-seven Jap planes in formation over the island – the swish of bombs. We stood there petrified, unable to fall to the ground. Then through the open door I saw two palm fronds floating to the ground. We laughed hysterically in relief.

Singapore Before the Japanese War

This was told to me by one of the Local Defence Force Volunteers. When transported as a POW to Thailand he saw his own car being driven about Bangpong. With a friend he entered the officers' club wearing a greasy uniform and looking rather disreputable. On their way to the changing room they encountered a high-ranking officer (maybe a general according to my note) who shouted officiously: 'Hoi! You're not allowed in here like that!'

His friend went across to the speaker and asked, 'Were you speaking to me?'

'Who the devil do you think you are, talking to me like that?' came the reply accompanied by violent explosions.

'I am the secretary of this club and have to see to good discipline.' The result was the general was suspended for three months.

Java Before the Japanese War

In Java cars with low registration number plates were given to high officials like the Governor General, the Viceroy, the Commander-in-Chief, the Mayor, etc. One man had 'D6' for his number and kept changing it to his new cars. The officials tried hard to take it from him because he was not a high-ranking official. He refused to agree and there was nothing they could do about it because there was no law on the subject. So the man rode round like a big pot.

Somewhere in England

The orderly room was where defaulters were dealt with in a time-honoured way. Military discipline was at its most rigid and adhered to under all circumstances. It must have been a very small company office as the bed (for the clerk on night duty) seems to loom large in the picture. The voice is that of the sergeant-major.

'Prisoner, hat off! Escort, accused and witness, right turn! Left wheel, quick march. Left, right, left, right, left, right, mind the bed, left, right, mark time, halt! Right turn.'

This tradition was faithfully upheld in the POW camps. When a man with ulcers on his leg hobbled into the orderly room at Changi, 'mark time' found him standing firmly on one leg raising the injured leg only in step with the escort.

Let us come back to England via Halifax in Canada. When Mac arrived there en route for Cape Town and the Far East he found nobody was to be granted shore leave. With two others he wanted to see Halifax, so putting battledress blouses over their PT kit they slipped through the barrier past a real 'Mountie' and found two girls standing by a lamppost. They were the first British

Tommies they had seen, and they thought the uniform (with the PT shorts) was cute. It happened to be a Sunday which may account for their impression that Halifax was a 'one horse' town. They were able to find a milk bar however. I'm glad to say they managed to get back to the ship without getting into trouble.

This same Mac told an amusing account of how they once got their Alsatian so drunk it could not stand up properly.

From Halifax in Canada to Halifax in Yorkshire. 'Les' described the very early days when his TA Field Regiment had no equipment. They practised gun drill using two chairs and a handcart to represent the gun. The following conversation takes place:-

Officer (with a perfectly serious face) to the man in the gun layer's seat: 'Laid on aiming point okay?'

Gun Layer: 'Yes sir! Left hand edge of drainpipe.'

Although the officer went through the motions of checking this with his eye glued to an imaginary dial-sight, he could not have seen the drainpipe because that happened to be on the outside of the building.

From Halifax to Leeds where an officer parked his car outside a pub while he went for a drink. When he came out there was a policeman minding his car. 'This your car?' The officer recognises the policeman as an old schoolmate.

'Yes, so what?'

'You're lucky! I've got a bet with my mate I'll run in more folk before Christmas than he does.'

'Well, give him my number then.' The officer drove off in his car, and I am still wondering who won the bet.

The gunner, who had been to a very good school had enjoyed the film. When the lights went up he saw a second lieutenant in the row behind who had been to the same school but was two years his junior. With great presence of mind, instead of saluting, he put out his hand and said, 'Nice to see you, Smith.'

Talking of bets brings me to this story. He was sitting in the bookmakers' office with seven or eight pals, all broke but knowing a 'dead cert'. Suddenly Ike had an idea. He said he wanted to take his slacks off to pawn but Lizzie is there playing on the pin-table. Lizzie was persuaded to disappear, then all except the teller of this story followed Ike's example. He didn't think his trousers were good enough but he obligingly took the others' slacks to the pawnbroker. The others all sat round in underpants until Ike could not stand the suspense any longer and went off to the lavatory, followed shortly by the rest. The narrator had nothing to lose so he waited to hear the result, which turned out favourable; but he could not resist telling the others the horse had lost. Everybody was in a blue funk for a little while but it all ended happily.

To slide further downhill, let us go from betting to drinking. This was told me by a sergeant. He went out with two pals deciding to make a night of it. They agreed to try every drink in the pub, including Drambuie. They spent more than five pounds. That night only one of them managed to get to bed. One fell down a slit trench and the other just lay on the floor. The sergeant (the fortunate one) crawled into his tent – then out again to vomit, a performance he repeated about six times during the night. Next morning, the sight of fat bacon sent him to the latrine at the double. When they drank tea at the morning break, it made them drunk again. Later, they tried strong canteen coffee but that did not help very much.

One of them was due to go on guard duty but was so incapable he had to pay a substitute five shillings. In the evening the sergeant tried a whisky as a pick-me-up with the result he was violently sick again. One of the others ate three eggs on toast and was violently ill. Altogether they were 'tight' for about a week.

They decided to work it off by kicking a rugby ball about but they just couldn't kick it. One of them even fell over in the attempt and went fast asleep on the ground. The sergeant couldn't face food for three days, taking only tea and coffee. He vowed in my hearing never to be so foolish again. I wonder if he ever was!

I've mentioned going on guard, so it is appropriate to mention other guard duty experiences. After a night manning a road block one lad was left behind to mind the heavy baggage until the lorry came. He was quite comfy in the tent and had nothing to do except wait. It was all right until one o'clock came and no one brought him any grub, and then he started to think he had been forgotten. He stopped an errand boy who happened to cycle by and asked him to take a note to the sergeant-major. 'Quite happy but hungry,' he wrote. An hour later the truck arrived. He *had* been forgotten.

'Bergy' of the Suffolks thought his worst guard was when he was on a petrol dump in some smugglers' caves. One man had to patrol through the caves and along paths with sheer drops to the sea, telephoning to the guardroom from various points as he went. At one point during the night he came out on a lawn where there was a white stone statue. This so scared Bergy that he nearly shot at it. It was a guard duty calculated to make you a nervous wreck.

And guarding petrol dumps brings us to Bill who came back from one claiming it was the first guard on which he had never smoked. (NB: smoking was prohibited on all guard duty.)

Darky was on guard in the open air beside an eight foot ditch near Stiffkey. Someone approached, not answering his challenge. He had been asleep and could not see too clearly. At his third challenge a cow poked her head in his face with a loud 'Moo!' The next thing Darky knew was he was the other side of the ditch, with his companion, Hector, laughing at him. The orderly officer came along just then and asked Darky how he had got across the ditch. 'I don't know, Sir.' He had to walk a quarter of a mile to go round by the bridge to get back to his post.

When Yorky was on guard he 'halted' a white horse the regulation three times and then fired. Fortunately he missed, which may have been due to his bad shooting or because of the darkness.

This same horse had cause to remember these lads for he was chased for two hours for a hair from his tail to tie round a wart on someone's nose. Three nights later the wart dropped off and the tent collapsed. The hair was blamed for both.

The Sergeant OC Guard told this one. One lad on the guard asked if he could go to the regimental dance. 'No!' Could he go round the corner for a drink? 'Yes.' He came back and again asked permission to go to the dance. Upon being refused he explains he has put three bottles of beer in the sergeant's pack. 'Okay then, you can go.' Another lad puts two bottles in his haversack and receives permission.

The orderly officer came in and found the sergeant and only two guards left (fortunately one was at his post). When told, in answer to his question, the others were round the corner playing darts with an officer in the pub, he smiled (apparently it was a practice winked at by those in authority) and murmured something about 'gone to the dance'. The sergeant assured him they all would be back before reveille. The officer leaves half a dozen bottles of beer and goes (presumably to the dance himself). In the morning there is a full guard and another regimental dance has been successfully weathered.

Another dance – for the battalion before they left the district. One lad meets a nice girl and dances with her. It appears she supplied most of the gramophone records for the music. He thought this was an excellent excuse for offering to see her home. She refused, saying the colonel was going to see her home, and adding, 'He often comes to our coffee and bun shop. He is such a dear.'

And girls bring us to the gallant 85th AT Regiment, and to Harry and Eric, who met two by arrangement one dark night. Harry told the girls Eric suffered from night blindness. They believed him and one girl took his arm and guided him along. Her solicitous 'Can you manage? This way, mind the step' embarrassed poor Eric but highly amused Harry. Eric soon got his own back however. They went to a dance. There was no band playing and Harry went up to the piano and trilled down the scale to create attention. They were short of a pianist so asked whether he could play. 'Oh yes.' Eric whispered something about 'BBC' and 'very good' and left him. Harry declined to play murmuring something about only playing for money (to save his face, I suppose). They offered to make a collection. I don't know what happened next.

He wanted to miss the route march so he could get out of barracks at four o'clock, and he knew the route march would get back after that time. So he decided to go sick with the toothache. The dentist made a mess of the job and got him a chit for 'bed down' for the rest of the day. No going out!

The CO decided to inspect the men just after leaving dugouts on the east coast. They paraded, muddy as they were, and the CO got no further than the front rank. In disgust he ordered a parade for the morrow; all cleaned, blancoed and creased. Strange as it may seem, blanco is not always white. In wartime it is usually khaki. It was scarce on this occasion and scrounging around produced five colours. The CO was not satisfied and ordered another parade – this time with 'squared packs'.

The Lost Train

We return to Malaya for this final story.

The train and the bridge were to be blown up before the advancing Nips. All was wired up but the bridge refused to blow. No one could understand why. One man volunteered to get up steam on the engine and run it onto the bridge where detonators were placed on the lines. The idea was for the vibration to set off the charges. Steam up, the train was got moving and the volunteer jumped clear.

Nothing happened and the train disappeared in the distance, heading for Singapore with a good head of steam. The bridge was never blown and the train was never heard of again.

How accurate these stories are I do not know. What is true is they passed the time pleasantly when there was nothing else we could do.

Appendix

Cyclopaedia Nunnica: Summary

This pompous title was chosen in a fit of humour for a notebook acquired soon after becoming a POW and kept hidden for three and a half years. The information it contains is not humorous for it shows the frustration of a student, his life brought to a standstill, but still possessed by the urge to gather any knowledge which might come in useful.

Some books I have read and what I thought of them

250 books read and commented on as a POW plus eighteen read on the journey out and on the way home. In the four years I was away that means I read one book about every six days. Often it was a case of 'beggars can't be choosers' with books, and some I would never have chosen under other conditions. I am glad to say Dickens, Scott, R.L. Stevenson, Thackeray, H.V. Morton, A.J. Cronin, Compton Mackenzie, Beverley Nichols and Agatha Christie featured among the authors.

A glossary of words I have met while reading

104 words defined when I met a dictionary, many with context.

Striking texts from books read

89 quotes (some quite long) plus a few references.

Useful data picked up here and there

Odds and ends of interest about the Bible

We live and learn – even in a prison camp
>Notes from lectures on the Himalayas and Cyprus; and from books about India, Japan (*Wings Over Asia*), the old Chinese empire, the weather, the history of painters, maritime matters (from *The Naval Side of British History*), the history of photography etc.

A few Chinese characters I've fathomed
Odd thoughts from the Bible
The Gospel – a skeleton address (sermon)
'Works' and 'witness' – two skeleton addresses
More addresses (sermons) – in note form
Thoughts on a conjuring trick
>It was awful and best forgotten!

Notes on vitamins – from a pharmacist's diary 1937–8
A few rules of Monopoly
Study of old English lettering
>Mainly, it seems, from the titles of newspapers

Study in lettering, my own opinions
'What a War!'
>Song by J. Moran based on A Troopship Leaving Bombay.

POW compositions – mad or otherwise
>The words of these and J. Moran's coming later

Some people I'd like to talk these days over with
>Unfortunately I never did

These things ought to taste good
>24 recipes from the sides of tins in Red Cross parcels

Notes on an attempt to learn German at Changi
Notes on Topham's' Company Law, 10th Edition
'Man' by Alexander Pope (lines 3–22)
'The Old Rugged Cross'
New names for old
>Familiar countries that have changed their names.

Some conventions of contract bridge:
The quickest way to lose friends is to play this game!
Russian Reconnoitre
Tunes for two Christmas carols
Notes on town planning etc. and traffic problems
En Route

Personal details of special events including clothing, 'credits' (the pay I hope to get when we are free), the kit washed overboard when sailing to Japan, details of Red Cross parcels (and there were not many of those).

Addresses (mini sermons) given while a POW
Publishers, authors etc.

And hints on style of writing.

Some books I would like on my library shelf

Including *The Desperate Pursuit* (Neil Bell), *Pictures Every Child Should Know* (American book), *No Place Like Home* (Beverley Nichols). The last one is the only one I managed to obtain.

Old English customs I've been told about

And quite a lot more not listed in the original index, such as a plan of the heavens and details about the planets.

'What a War': A POW composition by J. Moran

1. They say there's a trampship that's leaving Bombay
   But not bound for Blighty's shore;
   Heavily laden with a cargo of rice
   Bound for old Singapore.
   There's many an airman should be on this isle
   Taking his mess tin of rice;
   But they got into motion, and crossing the ocean
   They left us at – oh! what a price!

Chorus
   T'aint no joke! T'aint no joke!
   Things are not all 'oke doke'.
   Left on this isle in the hands of the Japs
   Makes us so mad 'cos they're all little chaps;
   But we'll soon say 'goodbye' to them all
   As back to their country they crawl:
   And then we'll get back on the old beaten track;
   So 'Cheer up my lads, do not fall!'

2. We'll never get used to this stuff they call 'rice'.
   The reason is plain to us all:
   Instead of home beefsteaks, we're now getting rice cakes
   On which we just manage to crawl.
   Don't think I'm the only one here with a grouse,

This grub is affecting us all.
But the time's not far hence when the world learns more sense,
And each man's put back in his stall.

3   There's one thing on which I am sure you'll agree,
Experience has taught us a lot:
Never to grumble when we get back home
At dinners which aren't quite so hot.
Last night I lay dreaming of my dear old home,
The table was laid very nice.
I pulled up my chair and began to dig in
When a voice bawled 'Fall in for your rice!'

A Mess Tin of Rice

I composed and sang this at a concert bearing in mind a Welsh national song.

1   The land of my fathers is far, far away,
        But there every mealtime my thoughts ever stray
        To a table so neat, piled with good things to eat,
        And never a mess tin of rice.

Chorus
        Rice! Rice! Bring me a mess tin of rice.
        Till death shall us part there will live in my heart
        A loathing, a turning from rice.

2   Please bring me fried bacon, tomatoes and eggs,
        Sweet tea with fresh milk and no tea leaves or dregs;
        A plate of boiled ham, and a dishful of jam;
        Instead of a mess tin of rice.

3   I want Yorkshire pudding, with gravy, of course;
        Green peas, baked potatoes, roast lamb and mint sauce;
        Fresh peaches and cream, for my 'afters' would seem
        More choice than a mess tin of rice.

4   There's trifle, fruit jelly, blancmange and iced cake,
        The sort of good things that promote stomach-ache.

> But I ask all in vain, and this thought brings me pain;
> I live on a mess tin of rice.

Living close together in a prison camp inevitably produced tensions, which prompted me to make up this couplet. It seemed so true.

> Whoever you be, you will surely agree
> Someone sees in you bad and concludes you are
> mad.